Go Get That Grant!

A Practical Guide for Libraries and Nonprofit Organizations

Gail M. Staines

THE SCARECROW PRESS, INC.
Lanham • Toronto • Plymouth, UK
2010

Published by Scarecrow Press, Inc.
A wholly owned subsidary of The Rowman & Littlefield Publishing Group, Inc.
4501 Forbes Boulevard, Suite 200, Lanham, Maryland 20706
http://www.scarecrowpress.com

Estover Road, Plymouth PL6 7PY, United Kingdom

British Library Cataloguing in Publication Information Available

Library of Congress Cataloging-in-Publication Data

Staines, Gail M., 1961-
  Go get that grant! : a practical guide for libraries and nonprofit organizations / Gail M. Staines.
    p. cm.
  Includes bibliographical references and index.
  ISBN 978-0-8108-7419-0 (pbk. : alk. paper) — ISBN 978-0-8108-7420-6 (ebook)
  1. Proposal writing in library science—United States. 2. Proposal writing for grants—United States. 3. Library fund raising—United States. 4. Nonprofit organizations—United States—Finance. I. Title.
  Z683.2.U6S73 2010
  025.1'1—dc22

                                                                    2009051834

∞™ The paper used in this publication meets the minimum requirements of American National Standard for Information Sciences—Permanence of Paper for Printed Library Materials, ANSI/NISO Z39.48-1992.

Printed in the United States of America

Contents

Acknowledgments

This text is a culmination of more than twenty years of writing and procuring grant funding for libraries and nonprofit organizations. One does not achieve success alone in the endeavors of grant writing. So, to that end, I would like to acknowledge several important individuals who have helped me along the way.

To Sheryl Knab, executive director of the Western New York Library Resources Council located in Buffalo, New York. Sheryl was instrumental in completing research and editing on several grants that were awarded full funding, making such projects as a virtual union catalog and a 24-7 online, interactive reference service—both situated in a multitype library consortium setting—a reality.

To the faculty librarians and library staff of the university libraries at Saint Louis University who support my work and the work of the university on a daily basis: Without their collaborative work ethic, we would not be able to achieve the high goals that we have set for ourselves and for the university libraries.

And to my family, most especially David and Ryan, who are always there, and to canine companions Missy, Emma, and Madeline: You all make life richly enjoyable!

1

Introduction

Libraries and nonprofit organizations traditionally rely on outside sources of funding in support of their mission. Whether it be financing a speaker series or renovating an older building, procuring monetary support is almost always a requirement for completing these projects. This is especially the case in times of heightened economic challenges, where a decrease in the availability of resources results in an increase in competitiveness to acquire those resources. The purpose of this text is to guide you through the granting process—from gathering basic information about your organization through accepting your grant award. Sprinkled throughout are practical examples and advice from the author's twenty-plus years of experience successfully writing grants.

WHAT ARE GRANTS?

A grant is a source of funding usually provided to one or more individuals or organizations. Grants are awarded upon acceptance and approval of an application requesting funding. Two types of organizations that offer grant opportunities are foundations and government agencies.

A foundation can be established by an individual, family, corporation, or group of organizations. Any individual or group can create a foundation through which they provide monetary support for programs and projects of strong interest to them. For example, a family may be interested in setting up a foundation to support activities that further the cause of clean water, reforestation, or early childhood education—the list of possibilities is endless. The individual or group can decide to support multiple interests such as health care, the arts, community beautification, and so on. A foundation needs to be established as a legally recognized entity, usually as a nonprofit corporation with a board of directors, mission statement, financial assets, permanent mailing address, and so forth before it can begin distributing funds.

Where does the money come from? An individual, family, or group of individuals can pool their money together. By law, a corporation may be required to set aside a certain amount of funds to be distributed annually. A regional community foundation may be responsible for managing and distributing funds from multiple foundations, acting much like a clearinghouse.

There is no set dollar amount required to be distributed through a foundation. An individual could create a foundation through which he or she gives out $100 per year. More often than not, however, individuals, families, and corporations start a foundation with a significant amount of funds (e.g., $1 million). The principle amount is maintained while the interest made on the principle is distributed in the form of grants. If the principle is $10 million, for example, and the interest made per year is $10,000, the foundation could decide to make the $10,000 available annually in the form of one grant or multiple grants with smaller dollar amounts.

The foundation's board of directors can also determine how frequently grants are awarded (e.g., quarterly, twice per year, annually), specify the life of the grant (e.g., one year, two years, three years), and decide whether or not to renew a grant. The foundation can also decide to stop awarding grants for a specific period of time. Even when applications are submitted, unless legally bound in some way, a foundation can decide not to fund any grant projects.

GRANTS FROM GOVERNMENT AGENCIES

Governments at all levels—federal, state, regional, and local—can decide to support specific projects through grants. According to the Office of Management and Budget, more than $16 billion was available to be awarded in 2008. Funding opportunities were available from agriculture to defense projects, energy and water development, to transportation and housing, just to name a few. Typically, the governing body (such as Congress or a county board of directors) determines the amount of grant funding to be awarded and the purpose for such awards. Frequently, grant funding supports a societal need that is perceived to be a priority, such as increasing the number of certified science teachers to teach biology, chemistry, and general science in public high schools, or keeping children engaged in learning through after-school programs. The identified funds are then given to a specific government agency that oversees the distribution of the grants. The agency will announce grant opportunities, the requirements for submitting an application, and the awards, as well as manage the funding, progress reports, press releases, and so on. The federal government announces grant opportunities in the *Federal Register* as well as via an interactive website, www.grants.gov. Other levels of government make opportunities known through various print and online publications. (See chapter 5: Funding Sources for more information on this topic.)

WHAT GRANTS ARE AND ARE NOT

Grants are funds given to individuals or organizations for a specific purpose to be completed in an agreed-upon time frame. Unless funds are misappropriated or misused, or if the unused portion of a grant is required to be returned to the granting agency or foundation, grant funds stay with the individual or organization that received the award. Grants are not loans to be paid back. Grant guidelines may tell you how the balance of any funds that remain after your project is completed are to be handled (e.g., returned to the granting agency or used for specific purposes). Then again, the guidelines may not address this issue. If you have concerns about disbursement of remaining funds, check with the program officer of the foundation or government agency for advice.

HOW MUCH MONEY IS AVAILABLE?

How much grant funding is available? The National Center for Charitable Statistics reports that:

- As of 2008, 112,959 private foundations were registered with the IRS (Internal Revenue Service).
- As of 2007, $283+ billion was given in the form of grants by individuals, foundations, and corporations.
- As of 2008, foundations awarded $45.6 billion. Of this amount, 72 percent was awarded by independent foundations, 10 percent by community foundations, and 10 percent by corporate foundations.

LEARNING FROM THIS BOOK

Each chapter of this book is dedicated to an essential part of the grant-writing process. Chapter 2 details the type of basic information you should have about your organization that will need to be included in most grant applications. Identifying a good project that is considered grant fundable is the focus of Chapter 3. Chapter 4 describes the more common types of grants that are available. Where you can locate government agencies and foundations that offer granting opportunities is provided in chapter 5. Grant writing is a very rigorous process, and Chapter 6 gives you practical advice on how to make your application stand out from the rest. Persuading others that your project or program is worth supporting monetarily is integral to successful grant writing, and this is the topic of chapter 7. Submitting a grant may sound easy, but there are some pitfalls to avoid and actions to take so that your application arrives before the deadline date. Some say that the real work begins once you accept the grant. Chapter 8 walks you through grant submission and grant implementation. Finally, additional advice and some final words on grant writing are offered in chapter 9.

If you are new to grant writing or have very little grant-writing experience, are a student who is required to compose a sample grant for a course, or are a seasoned author of grants who is looking for additional advice, then this book is for you. Even if you are not the grant writer per se but are involved in procuring outside sources of funding, this text provides you with an overall primer on the project selection through the grant acceptance and implementation process.

This book is especially useful for those writing grants on behalf of libraries as well as nonprofit organizations. The examples included in this book are geared toward government agency and foundation opportunities. If you are seeking funding for a science-based or social-science-based project that is an experiment and that may involve human or animal subjects, then this is not the text for you. There are many other books on grant procurement that are dedicated to the complexities of writing scientific grants, and you would be best served by consulting those.

Successful grant writing involves time, commitment, patience, and a good fundable project or program. I hope that you will come away with practical strategies for obtaining funding in this very competitive environment as I share over twenty years of successful grant-writing experience with you.

2

Creating Your Toolkit

Almost every grant application requires you to provide basic information about your organization. Chapter 2 provides you with the key pieces of information about your organization that are needed for most grant applications. It is a good idea to prepare a toolkit that contains the following information about your organization.

MISSION STATEMENT

Every organization should have a clear and concise mission statement that answers the question "What is our purpose?" For example, the purpose of an early childhood education center may be to educate and prepare children from the ages of two to four to enter kindergarten with basic skills. A sample mission statement for this type of organization might be: "Our mission is to provide excellent education to pre-K students to maximize their readiness for kindergarten." Here are other examples:

- The mission of the Niagara Falls Neighborhood Housing Services, Inc. is to be a leader in neighborhood revitalization, provide new housing opportunities for low- and low-moderate-income families, and serve as an advocate for community needs.
- The Buffalo Hearing and Speech Center provides comprehensive treatment for adults and children with speech-language and hearing impairments by integrating state-of-the-art technology with diversity, respect, integrity, positive relationships, compassion, and teamwork.

- Through a special partnership with horses, Fieldstone Farm Therapeutic Riding Center offers programs designed by professionals to foster personal growth and individual achievement for people with disabilities.
- The James Addison Jones Library serves the academic and social community that is Greensboro College.

You can see that a mission statement is very brief and to the point. It tells those who are not familiar with your organization exactly why your organization exists. Mission statements should be reviewed for currency and relevancy at least once each year.

ORGANIZATIONAL HISTORY

Another basic piece of information in your grant application is to describe, in as few words as possible, the history of your organization. Your institution might not even have a written history at all or might have a book-length explanation of its development.

If your organization does not have a written history, talk with current and former members; read through any archives (board meeting minutes, brochures, press releases, etc.) that might be available; search local newspapers to see if the institution ever appeared in the press; and search the Internet—you never know if someone has posted information that may be useful to you. As you and others piece together the organization's life story, remember to verify all the facts you include in its history. Members might recall a history that may or may not be accurate, so it is best to verify information before sharing it publicly.

If you have a lengthy history, your goal is to edit it down to no more than two or three brief paragraphs. This task can be hard work since the tendency is to include everything about the organization. However, grant reviewers do not have time to read extensive histories. Reviewers only want to read the highlights. It is your task to craft a brief paragraph that tells when the organization began, who established it, and why it was created. It is also good to include any major events, such as name changes, relocation, or significant alterations in mission. Below is an example of an organizational history.

> In the early 1970s, a group of fund-raisers established a Greater Kansas City chapter of what was then known as the National Society of Fund-Raising Executives, now the Association of Fundraising Professionals. When the chapter dissolved a few years later, several of the founders established a new group that they called the Greater Kansas City Council of Philanthropy.

In the early years, the council held meetings and events for fund-raisers to learn and network with peers. As the need grew among others in the nonprofit community to connect to training, resources, and networking opportunities, the council broadened its programs and services to serve them. Many of the programs and services evolved over the years to serve new needs and take advantage of new technology.

The Council on Philanthropy changed its name to Nonprofit Connect: Network, Learn, Grow, and unveiled its new website at www.npconnect.org on December 2, 2008. The new name and streamlined website enhances Nonprofit Connect's ability to serve nonprofit staff, community volunteers, business professionals and consultants, funders, and students. (www.npconnect.org/page/history, accessed 22 February 2010)

This example, albeit a bit shorter than many other histories of organizations, might still require revision if the grant application only provides for a one- or two- paragraph historical overview.

The organizational history you provide in a grant application plays a very important role. Like the mission statement, the history gives reviewers a clear view of who started the organization, why the organization began, and how it may have changed over time. It is recommended to have someone not familiar with the history read it prior to its final version. In this way, you will receive feedback as to how effectively you are communicating to someone unfamiliar with the organization—which is the perspective most reviewers will have when they read your grant application.

STRATEGIC PLAN

Whether or not you believe in strategic planning, grant reviewers want to see that your organization has goals and objectives, a business plan that supports these strategies, and measurable outcomes. From the simple to the complex, strategic plans should include, at the very minimum, at least three years' worth of goals and objectives, action steps, a timeline, budget, financial assets, and assessment measures. Plans also include a brief explanation of how assessment will happen continuously, so if outside events affect the organization, adjustments to the strategic plan can be made immediately.

Samples of strategic plans can be found in appendix A. For additional examples, check your local library or search the Internet. You can also ask similar types of organizations to share their strategic plan with you. Rarely is an entire strategic plan included in a grant application. Usually the request is to include a brief statement about the strategic plan with reference to how to access the complete version of the plan.

ADDITIONAL TOOLKIT INFORMATION

Along with the mission statement, brief organizational history, and strategic plan, funders almost always request the following information:

- A list of current board members, including officers
- Reference to updated bylaws
- Financial statement (known as the "990")
- Federal tax ID number

SERVICE POPULATION

Grant applications may ask you to briefly describe the population that the organization serves. This is another essential component of your request for grant funding and in your search for potential funders. Government agencies and foundations frequently support projects and programs that target specific demographics. For example, a grant for a summer fine arts program might only support a program for high school students located in an urban setting. Funding for children's health care might only support free dental care for low-income families. If your grant proposal does not meet the specific demographic requirements, do not spend time submitting your proposal to that particular government agency or foundation, as they rarely change grant guidelines to meet a proposer's request.

USAGE OF SERVICES AND PRODUCTS

Your toolkit should also contain information on the level of usage of the organization's services and products. This data is used to answer such questions as: How many people use this service? How frequently (once a day, weekly, monthly, etc.) is this service used? If the service is offered in multiple locations, where is it used the most? The least? How many products (e.g., books, CDs) have been sold, and how much revenue did the sales generate for the organization? Statistical data will tell the grant readers what areas of service are excelling and what areas require assistance.

Here is an example of effectively using data. Let's say you are applying for grant funding to purchase books for a specific library. Instead of saying "We need new books because the library's books are old," let usage statistics and other data tell your story. In this example, there are three libraries of similar size. Two libraries have high circulation counts, with people borrowing books continuously. Books are rarely borrowed from the third library. Your goal is to procure funding to purchase books for the third library.

One set of data you can use is the average copyright date of each library's book collection. (You can run copyright analysis on most library computer systems.) If the first two library collections have average copyright dates of the year 2004 and 2006 respectively, and the third library has an average copyright date of 1980 (twenty-plus years older), an argument can be made that the reason Library Three needs new books is that the books are too old. Library users go to the libraries with more current book collections. You can include the number of books borrowed from the three libraries as additional supportive hard evidence showing the need for funding.

Statistics—numbers—are not the only data you can use. Testimonials from individuals, both positive and negative, can be included in your proposal. People's comments about what they liked and what needs improvement put a face on your story. Here is one way to use testimonials in the proposal requesting grant funding for books:

> The statistics gathered show the need for Library Three to update its book collection. Library users have also voiced their opinions and concerns through a survey conducted within the past six months of the grant application. Library One received 50 usable surveys; Library Two received 48 usable surveys; and Library Three received 20 usable surveys. A total of 250 surveys were distributed and 118 usable surveys were returned for a return rate of 47 percent. (Note: Survey literature indicates that a response rate greater than one third [or 33-plus percent] should provide usable results).
>
> In the survey, library users were asked which library or libraries they most frequently used and why. Below are illustrative comments:

> "I would go to the library more often because it is closer to my house, but the book selection is too old!"—Long-time library user
>
> "Libraries One and Two have excellent collections! I usually find the book I am looking for."—Area businessperson
>
> "It seems that all three libraries in this community should have good current books to choose from. Two libraries keep their books up to date while Library Three has a horribly old collection. This needs to be fixed!"—High school student

You can see that putting words to numbers humanizes the need you are seeking to remedy. When using written feedback in your proposal, do not include the name of the person who provided the comments. This is done for privacy reasons. Age level, occupation, or other demographic information can be included as long as the completed survey cannot be traced back to the individual who completed the survey.

WHAT DO THE EXPERTS SAY?

Including references to quality information about existing needs or conditions related to your organization bolsters any grant application. Frequently, individuals are selected to be grant reviewers because of their education and experience in a topic related to the funding opportunities. Mentioning specific major articles, studies, books, and so forth shows the reviewer that you have gone above and beyond expectations by consulting recent as well as seminal works.

When deciding on the information to be included in your grant proposal, be very selective. Reference only the literature that is "on point" of your topic, that directly relates to your request for funding. List information that you know is reliable, timely, and accurate. For example, it is better to cite an article from a peer-reviewed journal, such as the *Journal of Sociology*, than a blurb from *People* magazine. Padding your list of references with articles and books tangentially related to your topic will not impress reviewers but will show them that you did not take the time to do an accurate search of the literature on your topic.

If grant guidelines allow, provide a list of references on a separate page. Follow a specific citation style, such as MLA (Modern Language Association) or APA (American Psychological Association), or just be consistent in the way you cite your resources. Reviewers, being well educated, are quite adept at reading citation lists for quality. If you need assistance doing a literature search, contact your local library and a librarian can assist you.

CONCLUSION

This chapter provides you with information frequently requested by grant funders. A current mission statement, brief organizational history, and an updated strategic plan are items to have handy anytime a grant application is completed. A list of board members, bylaws, financial statement (990), and the organization's federal tax ID number are frequently requested as well. Knowing the demographics of the population you serve, having both quantitative (statistical) and qualitative (evaluative) information about the services and resources you provide, and referencing relevant books and journal articles will be invaluable in supporting your request for funding.

3

Identifying a Project

This chapter will guide you in identifying a potentially fundable project. Specific strategies, such as conducting a needs assessment, establishing project goals and objectives, and writing tangible outcomes, are described.

SHOWING NEED

The best advice that can be given is: Don't make the project fit the grant. Grant reviewers can spot a grant application that has been molded to fit grant guidelines a mile away. Such grant requests usually do not read as being sincere. Have a sense of what you are seeking funding for and *then* select funding sources accordingly.

Once you have identified what you need financial support for, you can begin your needs assessment (or needs analysis). At this point, your organization should have completed a strategic plan that includes an environmental scan. Environmental scanning enables your organization to determine the strengths and weaknesses of your organization, the opportunities and threats from inside and outside your organization, and current trends and best practices in the areas your organization serves.

Many resources are available, both in print and online, that can guide you through the strategic planning process and how to effectively conduct an environmental scan. Your planning document should indicate the actions your organization should be taking to remain viable.

Using your strategic plan as a guidepost, brainstorm possible projects that require funding and that meet one or more goals of your organization. Funders will want to see that your application for funding is tied directly to your action plan. If you identify an activity to work on but you think that you need current input from the individuals who would benefit most from this project, then a needs analysis is in order.

Needs assessment means that you are gathering information that identifies and demonstrates that a true need does exist. Conducting a needs analysis ranges from the simple to the complex, using little or no financial resources to requiring monies and possibly hiring a consultant. How do you determine a need? There are several needs assessment methods that can be used individually or in combination. Surveys and focus groups are two of the more commonly used needs assessment tools. Each can be basic or intricate, and each can be implemented very cheaply or more expensively.

Surveys

There are many books and websites available on how to create a survey that will yield usable results. To create a survey online, Web-based survey services, such as SurveyMonkey.com, allow the responses to be submitted anonymously. It also enables you to retrieve an analysis of survey responses with a click of a button.

Whether you use a paper, phone, or electronic survey, there are some basic rules to follow when creating an effective survey.

- Make your survey short and to the point. (People do not like to wade through a lot of text to answer a question.)
- Keep the number of questions you ask to a minimum.
- Include a combination of multiple choice and short-answer questions.
- Test your survey on a small, representative group of individuals to determine whether or not you are obtaining usable information.
- Limit the time that the survey is available to complete, such as two weeks.
- Ensure that the responses remain anonymous, and convey this to the individuals completing the survey.

Overall, when developing your survey, think of whether or not you would personally complete the survey. If you would not take the time to complete your own survey, chances are no one else will either.

Focus Groups

Another needs assessment option that is commonly used is a focus group. Similar to surveys, focus groups can be arranged at a very simple level with little cost, to a professionally run focus group complete with videotaped transcripts. The advantage of doing a focus group is that you obtain immediate face-to-face feedback from the participants. If you find you need to modify questions asked or you want to ask additional questions, you are able to make those changes immediately. The goal here is to engage a targeted group of individuals to obtain input on the topics of your choice. You may invite people who already use your organization's services or people who do not use the services, or both. Whom you invite depends upon the type of information you are seeking to obtain. Do you want to discover ways to improve your services? Are you interested in finding out whether a new service is worthwhile to launch? Or do you want feedback on why people do not use your services?

Hosting a focus group or having a consultant host one for you is simple to arrange. At the minimum cost level, you can invite individuals by e-mail, electronic mailing lists, regular mail, or phone. Sometimes you will see announcements of upcoming focus groups on social networking spaces or Craigslist. If you have enough space, hold the focus group at your own organization. All you need are tables and chairs, some food and beverages (such as a continental breakfast, snacks, even pizza!), and a recorder. In the best of situations, it is also preferable to have the facilitator be a person who is knowledgeable about the organization, who can be dispassionate and impartial, and who does not have a vested interest in the organization. You are looking for open, honest feedback, so you need to avoid someone who may sway a participant's input one way or the other. The recorder can be anyone who is able to take clear and concise notes, capturing the essential content of the discussion. A focus group can last anywhere from one hour to more than three hours. Most run about ninety minutes to two hours with a short break in the middle.

The option at the other end of the spectrum involves hiring a consultant from a company that specializes in conducting focus groups. This option can be costly, in the range of several hundreds to several thousands of dollars. In return, you will receive guidance on what questions to ask and whom to invite. Frequently, companies will hold the focus group in locations where there are two rooms. One room is for the participants and has a one-way mirror. The other is for you and anyone else connected to your organization to sit behind the one-way mirror and observe the ongoing focus group discussion. A professional facilitator as well as a recorder will be provided. In this type of situation, the focus group may also be videotaped with a word-for-word transcript provided to you as well. The advantage of working with focus group experts is that (a) they know how to write questions that yield useable responses; (b) since you are watching the focus group in action, you can call the facilitator out and request that he or she ask particular questions; and (c) you have a verbatim transcript accompanied by a videotape to use afterwards. Additionally, a focus group final report that highlights themes should be provided by the company. Food and beverages, if ordered, will be billed to your account.

As with surveys, there are many texts and websites that can guide you through the focus group process. Consult these before doing a focus group or contracting with an expert or research company. In this way, you will be informed of any pitfalls to avoid and methods to use to have successful focus group outcomes.

WHAT ABOUT COMPENSATION?

Should survey and focus group participants be compensated for their time? The answer is not a simple "yes" or "no" but depends on each individual situation. Some argue that paying participants or providing them with some type of reward, such as a gift card or chance to win an item, gives people an incentive to complete a survey or actively engage in a focus group. Others argue that giving money or gifts is like bribing a person to participate and may result in the individual not providing usable answers. An additional important consideration is to check on whether there are any legal regulations that prohibit your organization from providing incentives. Does offering something in return for someone's time motivate him or her to partake in your needs assessment? This is a question to be seriously considered before offering any type of incentive.

PLANNING GRANTS

Planning grants provide monetary support to help your organization develop an action plan for the entire organization or for a specific project. For example, let's say that your organization has an archive of unique material about the history of your community. Located in several buildings around the city, the archive is in massive disarray. Some material is boxed, some organized into folders, and others just piled up in a room. Over the years, people have added all types of information to the collection, so the collection contains everything from photographs and videos to newspaper clippings, diaries, and other correspondence. Three-dimensional objects such as award plaques and old flags are also included. Collection management is also an issue, since similar items, such as newspaper clippings, were not added consistently over time. Your organization is interested in organizing the collection, preserving its contents in a safe environment, and developing a database of items digitized from the collection. In this example, a planning grant may be very useful.

Planning grants underwrite the cost of hiring experts to assist you in determining the best course of action for your organization or specific project. Such grants might also support the purchase of office supplies and rental of spaces to hold meetings. The deliverable at the end of a planning grant is usually a detailed action plan that includes estimated costs and a timeline for completion. Sometimes the same agency that provides a planning grant may require the submission of an action plan before you can submit a grant application to support the actual *implementation* of the plan. Other times, this is not a requirement. However, in most cases, there is no guarantee that you will receive funds to complete your project. Planning grants, like implementation grants, are frequently judged in comparison with other grant submissions and will go through the same competitive process.

CONCLUSION

Chapter 3 guides you through key elements of identifying a project that is potentially fundable. Grant reviewers want to see that your organization has done its homework by demonstrating that a need does exist for your project. There are various methods used to demonstrate need, including using survey and focus groups results. Focus groups can be conducted using very little money or can include hiring a consultant to professionally run a focus group for you, albeit at a higher cost. Whether or not your organization provides a reward (such as a gift card or cash) to focus group participants as an incentive needs to be determined by your organization. Reviewing relevant legal regulations may answer this question. Submitting an application for a planning grant may be useful if your organization's project requires expert assistance in project planning prior to seeking grant funding for implementation.

4

Types of Grants

Opportunities for funding are available for a variety of projects with a large range of monetary levels. Government and foundation funding is most frequently available for purchase of technological services or products, supporting professional development, underwriting the cost of programs, funding operations and construction or renovation, and for public relations and marketing. Some grants will fund only a portion of your proposal while other grants will financially support the entire package. This chapter provides you with information on the most common types of grants.

TECHNOLOGICAL SUPPORT

Funders that accept proposals to support technologies are usually open to the purchase of information technologies (IT). IT can include both hardware and software. Examples of hardware are computers (hard drives, monitors, keyboards, speakers), whether PCs or Macs, desktops or laptops; printers; physical connections to the Internet; the Internet service itself; digital projectors; 3D image projectors; SmartBoards; telecommunications peripherals such as flat screen monitors and Polycom units; and related supplies (ink jets, paper, etc.). Examples of software include the MS Office Suite (Word, Excel, Access), computer-aided design (CAD) programs, desktop publishing programs such as MS Publisher, and music creation programs. Funders may support the purchase of one copy of the software or multiple licenses so that the software can be accessed by several individuals. Depending upon the scope and purpose of your project, you may be able to acquire newer technologies such as iPhones, Blackberries, and e-readers.

For the most part, funders will support such technologies if they are used for new and innovative projects, such as integrating technology into instruction using various teaching methods or to design a different model for online course instruction. Funders may be open to replacing outdated technologies. However, IT used to administer a grant, such as an iPhone to do business or solely for personal use, frequently is not grant fundable.

In terms of funding IT, grant reviewers are looking for innovation and creativity. How is IT going to be used in a way that is different from other projects? What are your expected results? These are key questions that need to be answered in your grant proposal.

PROFESSIONAL DEVELOPMENT OPPORTUNITIES

Grants can support individuals to further their education, to broaden their expertise in a specific field of study, or to expand their knowledge in a new subject area. Professional development activities include attendance at workshops, seminars, and institutes (online or in person). Registration fees, travel, and lodging, along with additional fees such as lab fees or the purchase of materials required for the course, are usually grant fundable. Depending upon the grant guidelines, both individuals and groups may qualify for funding. Both credit and noncredit activities and programs that lead to certification can also be included.

Sometimes grant guidelines require that evidence of the knowledge obtained through a grant-funded activity be demonstrated. Evidence can range from submitting a press release to the media, to presenting at a conference, to submitting an article for publication. Providing evidence or reporting is not always required. However, if this is a stipulation, read the directions carefully as to what the expectations are and the deadline date for completion. Submit all required documentation, reports, and any other required information on time. This will keep you in good stead with the government agency or foundation you are working with, should you apply for a grant in the future.

PROGRAMS

In the world of nonprofit organizations and libraries, it seems that grant funding to support programs is the most prevalent form of grant opportunity available. Funders seem to lean toward making programs possible—programs that have the most promise toward creating a specific positive societal change. From literacy to early childhood education, from after-school programs to free dental care for children, the types of fundable program activities are wide ranging.

Grant applications that tend to be most successful contain the following elements:

- The program directly supports the mission of your organization.
- The program directly supports the mission of the grant funding organization.
- A target audience is identified.
- Specific activities are briefly described and may include:
  - Title of each activity
  - Potential presenters, with their qualifications
  - Number of people expected to participate
  - Location of each activity
  - A timeline of the entire program's activities
  - Evaluation of the program's successes and challenges
  - A plan for long-term sustainability of the program after funding ends

Grant applications that show a partnership with another organization, institution, or corporation, as well as demonstrating other sources of funding, either hard dollars or in-kind support, strengthen your request.

Here is an example of a request for funding a program: Pretend that you are the executive director of the Literacy Volunteers of Jamestown. The mission of your organization is to teach adults in your community how to read. In partnership with the local public library, volunteers of your organization have been working one-on-one with individuals. The organization is interested in expanding its reach to the rural areas of the community. Funding is needed to bring literacy programming to the people who need it the most. Your grant proposal seeks financial support for the purchase of reading materials, mileage reimbursement for travel to and from the new literacy sites, and marketing and information materials such as brochures, radio and TV announcements, and posters. This example might include the following elements of successful grant applications:

- Teaching adults how to read is the mission of your organization.
- You submit your application to funding agencies with a similar mission.
- Through census data and observations from area public libraries, you have determined that 15 percent of adults living in rural areas of your community do not know how to read.

- You are calling your overall program "Reading on the Road." Each activity underwritten by the grant will be branded with this phrase and a logo so that it is readily identifiable to the public.
- Trained literacy volunteers with the organization will be teaching adults how to read.
- It is anticipated that approximately thirty adults will participate in this program per public library. A total of five public libraries are partners in this grant, for a potential outreach to 150 adults.
- The program will be offered over a period of six months, according to the estimated timeline shown in table 4.1.
- You will evaluate the program's successes and challenges in terms of the number of people who participated and the reading level that each achieved.

For another example of a timeline, refer to chapter 6.

Table 4.1. Example Timeline of Activities

Activity Number	Time Frame	Activities
1	1st month	Receive grant. Send out press release announcing grant. Have public service announcements recorded. Have posters created and copied. Coordinate planning with organizations involved in the project. Create travel schedules and mileage reimbursement rates. Purchase reading materials.
2	2nd month	Send out public service announcements to radio and TV. Send out second press release to area media (print and online). Post posters throughout the community. Begin registration for literacy sessions at each library and online.
3 and 4	3rd and 4th months	Implement literacy education at all sites. Monitor for effectiveness and address any issues and concerns.
5	5th month	Complete program. Hold graduation for participants. Assess programs success (e.g., how many adults attended, how many can read at a certain level).
6	6th month	Press release announcing program results and thank grant funders publicly for their support. Reimburse mileage. Balance budget. Write final report to grant funder; include text on how you will continue to support the program into the future.

PLANNING GRANTS

Agencies and foundations may offer a category of grant known as a "planning grant." A planning grant assists you in developing an action plan that includes estimated costs and a timeline. The grant can be for your organization or for a project. For more information on planning grants, refer to chapter 3.

CONCLUSION

The most common types of grants are described in chapter 4. Funding is available to support technologies, including hardware and software. An organization can apply for grants that underwrite the cost of attending professional development opportunities. Probably the most prevalent type of grant available to nonprofit organizations and libraries is one that financially supports the development and implementation of programs that are designed for a targeted audience. Knowing the types of grants available will make the process of locating potential sources of funding easier.

5

Funding Sources

Locating sources of funding for your programs and projects is relatively easy and not at all complicated. It just requires some time searching electronic and print resources, then selecting a few good prospects to submit an application. This chapter provides you with informational databases, websites, and print sources that list government (state and federal) grants as well as grants offered by foundations.

START YOUR SEARCH

There is no one best place to start searching for granting opportunities, nor is there one perfect way to locate the information that you need. If you have completed a draft of a project plan that includes such information as what you want funded, why you need these funds, the impact that financial support will have on the population the project serves, and the amount of funding you need, then you are ready to begin!

GOVERNMENT GRANTS

Using the Internet, start by going to the website http://www.grants.gov. Overseen by the U.S. Department of Health and Human Services, grants.gov is *the* database to search for and locate federal grant opportunities. Started in 2002, this database enables you to also apply for a federal grant through this website as well as track the progress of your application.

The content on grants.gov is limited to grants from U.S. federal government agencies. Federal grants are not federal assistance or loans to individuals. As of August 4, 2009, more than 1,000 grant programs from twenty-six federal agencies are available via grants.gov. Categories of grants range from agriculture to education, energy to housing, natural resources to transportation, and everything in between. You can do basic searching by keyword, agency, category, Funding Opportunity Number (FON), and Catalog of Federal Domestic Assistance (CFDA) number. Additional options for limiting your search, such as deadline dates for grant applications and type of funding activity (such as arts or community development) are available. Each entry provides you with deadline dates, funding category, eligibility, expected number of awards, total amount of funding to be awarded, name of sponsoring federal government agency, a brief description of the grant, and a link to the full grant announcement. Most searchers enter a keyword to begin their search. Select a keyword or keywords that are unique to identifying your project. For example, searching the keyword "grant" in a grants database will yield hundreds of results. Your goal is to retrieve a manageable number of entries that you can skim through. Searching the keyword phrase "coastal marine," for example, is a specific search that will return several relevant entries. Sample entries for government grants can be found in appendix B.

American Recovery and Reinvestment Act of 2009

The intent of the American Recovery and Reinvestment Act (ARRA) (Public Law 111–5), signed into law by President Barak Obama on February 17, 2009, is to boost the U.S. economy by investing in various infrastructure projects and other societal programs. According to the American Library Association, there are three kinds of ARRA funding opportunities available for libraries: (1) infrastructure, (2) public computing centers, and (3) sustainable broadband adoption. Nonprofit organizations may also benefit from ARRA opportunities in the areas of arts and humanities, education, employment, job training, energy, housing and community development, and human and social services, to name a few. For additional information about ARRA and libraries, visit the American Library Association's website at http://www.ala.org. For more information about nonprofits and ARRA, visit the Council of Nonprofits website at http://www.councilofnonprofits .org.

Institute of Museum and Library Services (IMLS)

The Institute of Museum and Library Services (IMLS) is a federal government agency with the mission of creating "strong libraries and museums that connect people to information and ideas" (http://imls.gov, accessed 22 February 2010). According to imls.gov, this agency supports 123,000 libraries and 17,500 museums nationwide. Libraries include academic, public, and school libraries as well as graduate schools offering programs in library and information science, library associations, and library consortia. Types of museums are wide ranging and include historic sites, nature centers, and other nonprofits such as aquariums, planetariums, and zoos.

In 2009, IMLS offered grant opportunities in eleven categories: Twenty-first-century Museum Professionals, American Heritage Preservation Grants, Connecting to Collections: Statewide Grant for Both Planning and Implementation, Congressionally Directed Grants, Conservation Project Support, the Laura Bush Twenty-first-century Librarian Program, Museum Grants for African American History and Culture, Museums for America, National Leadership Grants, Native American/Native Hawaiian Library Services, and Native American/Native Hawaiian Museum Services.

In addition to directing federal granting opportunities, IMLS also oversees the Library Services and Technology Act (LSTA) of 2003 program. LSTA is a vehicle through which IMLS pushes federal funding to the states. Funds from LSTA can be used for statewide services or distributed via a competitive grant process. These activities are usually administered through each state's state library, which is located in the capital of each of the fifty states. The District of Columbia, Puerto Rico, Guam, American Samoa, the U.S. Virgin Islands, the Northern Mariana Islands, Marshall Islands, Micronesia, and Palau are also eligible to receive LSTA funds.

The IMLS website is very thorough; whether you are a beginner or a seasoned grant writer, the IMLS staff has provided you with information on searching for grants, a list of who is and who is not eligible to apply for grant funding, and instructions on how to submit your application. A sample application is provided online to help guide you in the grant-writing process.

Multiple search options are provided for you so that you can search by grant name, type of institution, and type of project. A list of previous grant awardees is also provided. This list can assist you immeasurably. Reading about the types of grants that have been awarded, including the amount of the award and the state where the project is located, is useful in helping you to determine if you have a fundable grant idea. So, if you are seeking funding for a library or museum, then IMLS is a great place to start.

State

At the time of the writing of this publication, there is no single source parallel to www.grants.gov for state grant opportunities. However, there are a few resources you can explore.

COS (Community of Science) Funding

Offered by COS (a subunit of the company ProQuest), COS funding is a searchable database of grant funding opportunities (www.cos.com) available worldwide, including local government agencies and private foundations. Opportunities are listed for almost all disciplines (e.g., social sciences, life sciences) and support a variety of activities such as curriculum development, conferences, travel, equipment, capital and operational expenses, and more. A number of search options are available including keyword, geographical, and sponsoring agency. COS funding is available for subscription by small businesses and institutions such as colleges and universities, libraries, government agencies, companies, and nonprofit organizations. Because individual subscriptions are not available, check out the website of your local library or that of your employer to see if access is available to you.

SPIN (Sponsored Program Information Network)

A product of InfoEd International, SPIN gives you access to grant postings provided from more than 6,000 private, nonprofit, public, and government agencies, including state grants. Like most databases, SPIN can be searched by keyword, sponsor's name, program number, deadline dates, and more. Available by subscription only, check with your local library or employer for access (http://www1.infoed.org).

Locating grants offered by states can also be found through subject-specific sites. For example, the Database of State Incentives for Renewable Energy (http://www.dsireusa.org) provides information about incentives available for promoting energy efficiency and renewable energy. Searching is made easy via a clickable map of the United States as well as by type of technology, type of incentive (such as tax incentives, loan programs, and grants), and type of agency or institution. This resource is funded by the North Carolina Solar Center and the Interstate Renewable Energy Council. Additional subject-specific sites can be found by searching the Internet using the terms: +*grants* +*state* + [typing in the subject area you are interested in here]. For example, searching +*grants* +*state* +*education* will retrieve many sites where you can find education grants offered by specific states.

Another strategy for locating grant opportunities by state is to visit your state's main government website. Through the state website, you can look at specific state government agencies that offer grants. For example, if you are looking for education grants, visit your state's Department of Education webpage. If you are searching for housing grants, look for a Department of Housing website.

Remember that grants offered by a specific state are almost always awarded to an institution located within that state and are sometimes only available to those located in a specific region or city within that state. There are always exceptions, and you may find a grant offered by two or more states or a region (e.g., Northeast), but this is not the norm. As a timesaver, search for funding opportunities only within your state. Odds are in your favor for receiving a grant from the state where your institution or organization resides.

FOUNDATIONS

Receiving a grant from a foundation is another way to obtain monies for your organization. Community foundations, corporate giving programs, and grant-making public charities are types of foundations. Corporations of all kinds have foundations, including industries, banks, grocery stores, office supply stores, and so on. Nonprofit foundations are usually a result of a family or individual creating a way to provide funding to society by establishing a foundation. Rotary clubs and greater regional councils often offer foundation grants, too.

Locating sources of funding from foundations is similar to searching for other types of funding. A quick way to start your search is to type in the name of a specific foundation into any Internet search engine. You can also search the Internet by subject as shown in the following two examples:

+foundation +grants +housing
+foundation +grants +teaching

You can further refine your search by adding the state where your organization resides:

+foundation +grants +housing +Missouri
+foundation +grants +teaching +Iowa

Many foundations do have their own websites, although some do not.

Another source you can search is www.foundations.org. This free website is provided by the Northern California Community Foundation, Inc. Here you will find an alphabetical list of corporate and private foundations with links to websites (if available) as well as a schedule of upcoming workshops on grant writing.

Foundation Directory Online

This resource is available by subscription through the Foundation Center. Information includes the name of the foundation and contact information, grant amount, types of support, and similar data. Database content is culled from IRS forms 990 and 990-PF returns, websites, annual reports, and other sources. Entries are primarily for organizations seeking grant funding, although the Foundation Center offers a separate database for individuals called Foundation Grants to Individuals Online. The database is searchable by name of foundation, name of company, keyword, and so on. At the writing of this book, a subscription to the Foundation Directory Online was $19.95 per month. Check with your local library to see if they provide access to this resource.

The Chronicle of Philanthropy Guide to Grants

This online resource provides access to foundation, corporate, and nonprofit grant opportunities. Searchable by subject, name of funder, and name of awardees, entries include information regarding grant amounts, deadline dates, and brief descriptions by grant opportunity. The subscription per year at the time of the writing of this book was $49.00 per year. Check with your local library for access.

GuideStar

Founded in 1994, GuideStar (www.guidestar.org) is a searchable database of information about 1.8 million-plus nonprofit organizations. Nonprofits can submit information about their organization, such as mission statement, staff information, contact information, financials, needs, and so forth at no cost. Registration and searching is free, although membership and donations are encouraged; premium access is also available per paid subscription.

Philanthropy Journal

Found at www.philanthropyjournal.org, this free Web-based resource is a portal to a wide range of information regarding philanthropy. Current news, articles on fund-raising, job postings, and links to additional sources of funding opportunities are provided.

Print Resources

You may find current directories of foundations on the shelves of your local library. Such directories include information similar to that found online: title of foundation, contact information, grants awarded, and so on. Print resources are a good starting point to identify potential funding prospects. Since the lag time in printing a directory in book form can be six months or longer, it is recommended that you verify the information online or by calling the foundation office directly.

CONCLUSION

The focus of this chapter is to provide you with resources that contain grant-funding opportunities. How to locate federal and state government grants as well as those available through public and private foundations are described. Specific electronic databases and websites—both free and fee-based—along with print resources are provided.

If you know what you are seeking funding for, can succinctly explain why you need these funds, and can predict with some certainty the impact that financial support will have on your target population, locating several grants applicable to your project should be relatively easy.

As with all searches for any type of information, if you are not finding what you need, contact your local area library and ask a librarian for assistance.

6

Select a Grant and Start Writing

Completing a grant application—writing persuasively so that your project will be funded—is possibly the most challenging aspect of the entire grant process. This chapter gives you important questions to consider while completing the grant application, as well as specific tips on the art of writing a successful grant.

GRANT GUIDELINES

It cannot be overstated that you need to read the grant guidelines very carefully. Failure to address each grant application requirement will likely result in the rejection of your application. It is also best to carefully read through the grant application and any accompanying directions or information before you begin the writing process. In reading through this material, you may find that your proposal does not meet specific requirements or that you need to provide additional information.

If a government granting agency or foundation offers an information session or workshop on how to write for a specific grant opportunity you are interested in, attend! This is a superb way to ask questions and to hear the questions and answers from other potential applicants. You will also have the opportunity to personally meet the project director or grant manager. If the grant is a major federal government program or a significant large grant offered by a major foundation, you might find these types of presentations given as part of a national conference or offered at various locations around the country or online as a webinar. Attending such sessions will provide you with additional key points to make in your proposal.

Another way to seek additional information about current and upcoming funding possibilities is to visit your federal, state, or relevant government representative in his or her home office. When making an appointment, be specific about the reason for your visit. Sometimes you will meet with an aide to the representative. Each aide is assigned an area of responsibility (education, social services, etc.) and will meet with the representative after completing research and meeting with constituents. The aide will present a summary of your meeting to the representative. It is a good idea to stay in touch after your initial visit by sending press releases and other newsworthy items about your organization to the representative's office. Your government representative will be more apt to remember you when a grant possibility arises and may, if allowable by grant guidelines, write a letter of support for your proposal.

MATCHING GRANTS

There are also a few specific requirements that almost all applications should address and that you should be familiar with. You should know whether or not the grant is considered a "matching grant." Matching grants require you to show evidence that you have the resources available to support identified items. For example, one-to-one matching grants usually insist that, for every dollar you are requesting, you have another dollar to match. If you are asking for $100,000, then you need to supply evidence that you have $100,000 available to you to match your financial request.

There are different variations of matching in grant applications. It could be 60/40 (or any percentage thereof), where the grant will pay for 60 percent of the cost of the entire grant or a portion of the grant and your organization needs to pay for the other 40 percent. *In-kind support* matching grants also exist. Here, your organization provides a match to a designated amount per grant requirement—only the match is not in hard dollars but in what is referred to as "in-kind" support. Examples of in-kind support are rent, supplies, staffing, and so on. It must be shown in the grant application that the in-kind support you list is directly tied to supporting your proposal. Let's say you are requesting $25,000 to offer a lecture series in your public library. The amount you are requesting ($25,000) will underwrite the cost of the travel, lodging, meals, and honorarium for each invited presenter. In turn, the public library will match the $25,000 in terms of in-kind support as follows:

- 20 percent of the library administrative assistant's salary for grant oversight (scheduling presentations, completing travel arrangements, lecture room setup, etc.)

- supplies (such as posters, mailings, postage)
- technology (e.g., microphone, computer, and video display unit)

In-kind support tells the grant reviewers that your organization is not committing hard dollars to this project but that you are supporting its success in terms of tangible resources that have a dollar value.

QUERY LETTER

Foundations, more often than government agencies, may require you to submit a query letter before submitting a complete grant application to them requesting funding. Such a letter saves you time in completing a grant application and saves the foundation time reviewing an application that may not fit the foundation's funding goals.

The purpose of a query letter, also known as "a letter of inquiry" or a "letter of intent," is to provide the reader with a brief explanation of your organization and your project. Traditionally, this letter is no longer than two to three pages and includes the following important elements:

- A brief explanation of why you are submitting the query letter
- A brief history of your organization, its mission, successful programs, and current plans
- Key staffers with their education and experience
- Names of influential/prominent board members
- Amount of funding you are seeking
- Brief overview of your project
- The positive impact your project will have on a specific group
- An explanation of why your project needs to be implemented; include quantitative and qualitative information if possible
- The connection of your organization's and project's goals with the foundation's mission; be sure to answer the question: How does the project further the foundation's goals?
- A description of the role of your organization in the project in terms of public relations, marketing, collaborating, and mutual benefit to both organizations
- Confirmed financial or other support from other sources (if applicable)

In closing the letter, summarize the project, provide additional relevant information if necessary, include next steps, and then thank the foundation for its time in considering your request. Include contact information of one individual from your organization. This is usually the executive director.

Have your letter signed by the executive director or the president of your board. Unless otherwise noted in the query letter guidelines, do not include any additional information or documentation.

Once you submit a query letter, you should hear back from the foundation within a reasonable amount of time. The response will typically be to submit a complete application, to submit an application with suggested changes, or you will receive a rejection notice. Whatever the response, always thank the foundation for considering funding your project. For a sample query letter, see appendix C.

DEVELOPING A REALISTIC TIMELINE

Another essential element of successful grant writing is establishing a realistic timeline of activities. The tendency here is to overload the timetable with too many activities in a very short period of time. Your goal is not to impress grant funders with the amount of work your organization can accomplish but rather to show others how you are going to use their funds judiciously by applying their support to solid activities that lead to effective results. In other words, quality, not quantity, is essential to building a realistic timeline.

What is the best way to present your timeline? Unless otherwise indicated in the grant guidelines, activities are usually presented in chart form in the order that the activities are performed and the length of estimated time it will take to complete each activity. The length of time is usually expressed by the number of months or quarters of a twelve-month time period. Rarely are specific dates included unless confirmed. Table 6.1 is an example of a realistic timeline of activities for a speaker series. (For another example timeline, refer to table 4.1.)

Presenting grant activities in this manner enables you to easily transfer the timeline to another grant proposal should your initial attempt to procure funding is not successful.

Where does one begin in developing a calendar of activities and action steps? Do you always need to start with the first activity being the receipt of the grant? It is not necessary to always start your timeline with "receiving the grant." In fact, listing previous work that has already been completed toward the project shows the reviewers that some research and preplanning has occurred prior to grant submission. Using the above speaker series example, this timeline could be modified to show work completed to date.

When developing a timeline of activities for your grant application, take care to thoroughly think through what you and your organization can reasonably accomplish in the brief period of time that most grant guidelines allow you to complete your project. Quality activities should enable you to

Table 6.1. Second Example of a Timeline of Activities

Activity Number	Time Frame	Activities
1	1st month	Receive grant. Send out press release announcing grant. Confirm dates, times, locations with speakers. Confirm locations of presentations.
2	2nd month	Mail contracts to speakers. Sign contract with presentation locations. Confirm speakers' presentation needs. Confirm presentation title, obtain short description and biography. Confirm presentation needs with location.
3	3rd–5th months	Do ongoing marketing and public relations (e.g., press releases, media contacts announcements) Record number of people in attendance at each event. Distribute and gather speaker evaluations at each event.
4	6th month	Complete all necessary paperwork, including financial commitments. Write final report; include such information as number of presentations, attendance, analysis of evaluation responses, overall plusses and minuses of events, and recommendations for future events. Summarize survey responses and send to each presenter.

complete tasks on time and on or under budget. Too many activities may result in some not getting finished. It is better to complete a few grant-funded activities successfully than to promise to finish a number of activities only to discover that there was too much to accomplish in the timeline you established for yourself and your organization. Grant funders remember projects that fall short of promised expectations as well as the grant project directors responsible for such failures. Be conscious of this and work to build a solid reputation for successfully completing grant projects.

DEVELOPING A REALISTIC BUDGET

Crafting a realistic budget—one that will enable the goals and objectives of the grant to be met—can be a real balancing act. On the one hand, revenue and expenses need to be such that the grant-funded project can occur without going over budget. On the other hand, listing everything you want to accomplish and acquire will be viewed by grant reviewers as a "grab for all the money you can get" application that would most likely not be funded. Thus, developing a realistic budget will take some time for cost comparisons and calculations.

Grant guidelines specify what is fully grant fundable, partially grant fundable, or not fundable at all. The levels of funding you may request are also grant specific. Read the guidelines carefully before creating your budget, as you may find that one grant may provide funding for a certain activity while another will not. For example, one grant may fund full-time staff while another will only support an employee part-time. Because budget requests are grant-guideline specific, this section will provide you with overall general advice for developing a realistic budget.

Draft a List

When starting on your budget, make a list of all the costs related to the goals, objectives, and activities of your project. At this stage, do not be concerned with identifying where the money is or will come from. This exercise is to delineate all the monetary costs needed for your project.

Using the example of requesting funds to underwrite the cost of a speaker series, table 6.2 could be used as a basis for developing a budget.

Calculating Costs

The next step after completing your initial list of related costs is to verify each budget figure. Obtain three quotes for each item. Calculate the average cost of all three quotes. This is a frequently used method for estimating budget figures. For example, if you think the cost of printing one color brochure is $1.00, but you are not completely confident, contact three printers

Table 6.2.   Sample Budget List for Speaker Series

Item(s)	Estimated Cost
5 presenters × $100 honoraria per presenter	$500.00
Travel, food, lodging allowance:	
$200/presenter × 5 presenters	$1,000.00
Publicity	
Design and print 500 color brochures @ $1.00 per brochure = $500.00	
Mailing of brochures = $500.00	$1,000.00
Room rental	
5 presentations × $100/room	$500.00
Audio/Visual Equipment Rental	
A/V for 5 presentations × $50 for equipment	$250.00
Evaluations	
Printing of 500 evaluations × $0.50/evaluation	$250.00
Refreshments	
$50/presentation × 5 presentations	$250.00
TOTAL	$3,750.00

and request price quotes. Receiving three different quotes is common. All you need to do is take the average cost of the three quotes and use that figure in your budget.

As you work to finalize your budget, be aware of any potential hidden costs. For example, does renting audio/visual equipment for each presentation include any setup charges? Do printing costs include a design fee? Can the brochures be printed with addresses, or will you need to purchase and affix mailing labels? When reviewing your budget, think about all of the components of each activity involved in your entire project. Walk through each part of your grant, making sure to mentally identify all the details needed to make the project a success. Through this exercise, you should be able to determine all costs associated with your project.

Presenting the Budget

How the budget is presented in the final grant application is dictated by the grant guidelines. The guidelines may request a list of items and associated costs. Sometimes this list is accompanied by a brief narrative that explains the purpose of each item. Here is a sample budget narrative:

Sample Budget Narrative for Speaker Series

Honoraria: $100/speaker × 5 speakers = $500

Each speaker will receive an honorarium in the amount of $100 upon completion of a one-hour presentation on an agreed-upon topic.

Travel/Food/Lodging Allowance: $200/speaker × 5 speakers = $1,000

Each speaker will be allocated a $200 allowance to be used for travel (mileage reimbursement at current federal reimbursement rate, flight, train), food, and lodging connected with grant-funded presentation. Reimbursement is payable upon submission of receipts.

Publicity: Design and print 500 brochures × $1.00/brochure = $500

Mailing 500 brochures = $500. Total cost = $1,000

Five hundred color brochures announcing the speaker series and including a photograph and brief biography of each speaker will be produced and mailed at a total cost of $1,000.

Room Rental: $100/room × 5 presentations = $500

Each of the five presentations will be held at the ABC Conference Center. Cost of $100 includes room setup and cleanup fee.

Audio/Visual Equipment: $50 for equipment/presentation × 5 presentations = $250

The ABC Conference Center will provide a podium, wireless microphone, screen, computer, and digital display unit at a cost of $50 per presentation. The ABC Conference Center is including audio/visual setup free of charge.

(*continued*)

> *Sample Budget Narrative for Speaker Series (continued)*
> Evaluations: 500 evaluations printed at a cost of $0.50/evaluation = $250
>   One hundred evaluations will be made available at each presentation. Evaluations will be gathered and responses analyzed at the conclusion of the speaker series.
> Refreshments: $50/presentation × 5 presentations = $250
>   Light snacks and soda will be provided at each presentation at a cost of $50 per session.

Depending upon the grant guidelines, the itemized budget and narrative may be combined into one section.

Showing Other Resources

Again, depending upon the grant guidelines, the application may require you to show additional sources of funding as well as any level of in-kind support. Demonstrating that you have already obtained financial support from other sources tells the reviewers that efforts have been made toward making your project a reality. Indicating that your organization will provide some level of in-kind support shows the foundation or government agency that your organization is willing to provide services and resources necessary to implement the project successfully (see table 6.3).

Other Financial Resources

Grant guidelines may explicitly state how and where to include additional sources of financial support. Here is an example of how to communicate to grant readers that other sources of funding have been confirmed or are in the process of being confirmed.

> *Sample Narrative*
> Our project includes hosting a series of lectures on the topic of literacy in America. Each of five presenters will receive a $1,000 honorarium. We have secured $1,000 from Excelsior Bank, a local financial institution, and we are waiting for confirmation from the Regional Community Foundation of support in the amount of $1,000. We are requesting $3,000 so that we have a full complement of speakers.

Showing In-Kind Support

In-kind support is frequently a requirement of grant proposals. Why? Providing some level of your organization's services and resources tells the

Table 6.3. Estimated Costs and Funding

Items	Estimated Cost	Funding Secured	Funding Forthcoming	Funding Requested
Honoraria for 5 presenters @ $1,000/presenter	$5,000	$1,000 from Excelsior Bank	$1,000 from the Regional Community Foundation	$3,000

reviewers that your organization is serious about the project and shows your willingness to partner your resources with those of the agency or foundation.

Administrative support, such as attending to correspondence, updating Web information, sending out press releases, and so on is frequently a requirement of grant proposals. Other examples are providing supplies such as postcards, postage, mailing labels, and paper. Read the grant guidelines to see if certain types of in-kind support can be included in your application, as well as to determine those that are excluded, if any.

Having your staff members contribute part of their workday to a grant-funded project is quite common. Reviewers look for any experience or education of the employee that directly relates to the proposal. For example, if your program manager is also going to serve as the project director, connect his or her essential experiences with managing grant projects. Refer the reviewer to an updated resume of the employee, which is usually appended to the grant application.

In-kind support is frequently a separate section in a grant application. You will need to append a dollar value for each item listed as "in-kind." Some examples of how to determine the monetary value of some of the more common in-kind support items follow.

Calculating Percent of Salary

Including a percentage of staff members' salaries as support for your project is often shown as in-kind support. For example, let's say that your project requires a project director as well as administrative support. The project director, a member of your organization's staff, is going to spend approximately 25 percent of his or her time managing the project. To convert time into dollars:

1. Add the person's yearly salary and benefits (if benefits are provided) to obtain the total salary and benefits for one year.
2. Take the total salary and benefits and multiply by 25 percent to calculate the dollar amount of in-kind support.

Here is a sample calculation:

1. $50,000 annual salary + $16,500 benefits = $66,500
2. $66,500 × .25 = $16,625

In your proposal, you would list $16,625 as the amount of in-kind support your organization is providing for the project director's position. You would go through the same calculation to determine the dollar amount for administrative support.

Note that there is no hard and fast rule indicating the exact percentage of a staff member's time to be allocated toward the project. With staff input, estimate the time each staff member will dedicate to the project and then calculate accordingly. In addition to their time, you can estimate the dollar value of the office space used. To do this:

1. Determine the square footage of the staff member's office or work space.
2. Divide your organization's monthly rent or mortgage payment by the total number of square feet you rent or own to obtain a per square foot cost. You can also add monthly utility costs such as heat, electricity, and Internet access to the monthly rent/mortgage amount and use this total amount in the formula accordingly.
3. Multiply per square foot cost by the number of square feet of the office/work space.
4. In this example, 25 percent of a person's salary and benefits will be dedicated to managing this project. You can then calculate 25 percent of that person's office/work space usage and include this figure in your grant application. In this example, you would multiply the total square footage cost of the office/work space by 25 percent to obtain the in-kind rent/mortgage figure for the grant.

Here is a sample calculation:

80 square feet of workspace
$1,000/month for rent, utilities, etc.
8,000 square feet = building size
8,000 square feet/$1,000 monthly expenses = $8.00 per square foot
$8.00 per square foot × 80 square feet workspace = $640.
$640. × .25 = $160. in kind support per month for project
$160. × 6 months of project = $960.
$960 × 2 employee's workspace on project = $1,920.

The type of in-kind support you can use is dependent upon the grant guidelines as well as on the needs and requirements of the project. Common in-kind support services are managerial support, administrative support, and information technologies (IT) support. In-kind items include such resources as office supplies, advertising, and Web design.

Reviewers appreciate an application that shows in-kind support visually and narratively, if the grant guidelines allow. Using the example above, table 6.4 clearly indicates the types of support you have as well as the support you are requesting.

Here is a sample narrative that accompanies the above example.

Costs
Honoraria: 5 presenters × $1,000 = $5,000
Five presenters participating in this project will receive an honorarium in the amount of $1,000 each, for a total of $5,000.
Funding: Outside funding = $2,000
Excelsior Bank has contributed $1,000 to this project. The Regional Community Foundation has agreed to contribute $1,000. We are requesting $3,000 to complete needed financial support.
In-Kind Support
The Literacy Volunteers of Jamestown will provide the following in-kind support:
Project Director = $16,625
It is estimated that 25 percent of the Literacy Volunteers of Jamestown assistant director's time will be spent serving as project director for this project. The project director has five years' experience in managing similar programs. (Please see enclosed resume.)
Administrative Support = $6,250
It is estimated that 25 percent of the Literary Volunteers of Jamestown executive assistant's time will be spent supporting this project in terms of correspondence, scheduling meetings, making travel arrangements, and similar duties.
Office Space × $1,920.
Office Supplies = $500.
Literacy Volunteers of Jamestown will provide envelopes, letterhead, and postage for this project.
The total amount of in-kind support is $25,295.

A WORD ABOUT SUSTAINABILITY

One of the more challenging sections of a grant application is explaining to the grant funders your plan to continue offering the work you started under the grant itself. Government agencies and foundations may not be interested in how or if your project will continue once funding ends. Some

Table 6.4. Types of Outside and In-kind Support

Items	Estimated Cost	Funding Secured	Funding Forthcoming	Funding Requested	In-Kind Support
Honoraria for 5 presenters @ $1,000 per presenter	$5,000	$1,000 from Excelsior Bank	$1,000 from the Regional Community Foundation	$3,000	
Project director	25% of assistant director's time				$16,625
Administrative support	25% of executive assistant's time				$6,250
Office space					$1,920
Office supplies	Envelopes, letterhead, postage				$500
			Total in-kind support		$25,295

grant-funded projects simply end within a specific time frame with no expectation for continuation once the grant stops. However, applications may require you to address the continuation of your work efforts after the grant is over.

If this question is asked by the government agency or foundation, seriously think about what your organization will and will not be able to do once funding ceases. Depending upon your organization's situation, you can consider responding to the issue of sustainability in different ways. Here are some example responses:

- Our organization will continue to search the Internet, databases, and electronic mailing lists as well as network for various funding opportunities both during and after this project ends.
- A year before the grant is over, our organization will work on procuring funding through such activities as hosting fund-raising events, submitting applications for other grant opportunities, and exploring partnership with area organizations to continue our program.
- Our organization will seek a dollar-for-dollar match to our organization's project fund from local area foundations.
- We will continue offering our programs by charging a cost-recovery fee for services provided.
- Individuals educated through our "train-the-trainer" program will continue teaching others, thus continuing the work begun under this grant project.
- Grant participants will share their knowledge and experiences gained from this project through presentations, workshops, Web blogs, and similar ventures.
- Grant participants have agreed to establish a website that will list relevant information. (Note: If you decide to implement this as a way to sustain your project, make sure that you have a plan in place to update the information on a regular basis. You want to avoid having dated or incorrect information on a website with your organization's name tied to it.)

BUDGETING FOR EVALUATION

Depending upon the grant application, you may or may not be required to provide a plan for how you are going to evaluate whether or not you reached the goals of your project. Evaluation plans are almost always a component of any grant application for federal funding, but less so for foundation grants.

What Is an Evaluation Plan?

An evaluation plan is similar to the needs assessment process described in chapter 3. As you used such tools as surveys and focus groups to determine the need for your program, the evaluation plan is often implemented toward the end of the grant project. Also similar to the needs assessment process, cost of an evaluation plan can range from a plan on a shoestring budget to one that costs several thousands of dollars.

To create and implement the evaluation plan on a small budget, you will essentially follow the needs assessment process as outlined in chapter 3. At minimum, you can survey project participants via regular mail, e-mail, phone, or (the most popular form) a Web-based survey. You can interview project participants in person or via phone. And you can also schedule a focus group to gain participant feedback.

With a larger budget, you can use each of these evaluation instruments by outsourcing surveys, interviews, and focus groups to an evaluation consultant. Sometimes grants will require you to hire an external evaluation consultant. The reason behind this third-party approach to evaluation is that the process should be more objective if performed by an uninterested party rather than the project leaders themselves. The actual leaders may be seen as having a vested interest in the success of the project. As a result, the evaluation results may be more subjective and skewed toward the positive rather than being neutral or pointing out the challenges. Granting agencies may allow you to pay for third-party evaluators through the grant. Read the grant guidelines carefully in regard to this item.

What Are You Evaluating?

What are the expectations of an evaluation plan? Unlike a needs assessment where you are determining the level of need for a specific resource or service by a target audience, an evaluation plan (sometimes also referred to as an assessment plan) seeks to answer such questions as: To what level have we achieved the goals identified in this project? In what areas of the project were we not successful and why? Did participants' skill levels change? If so, to what degree did they change?

Through the evaluation process, you will gather both qualitative and quantitative information. Surveys with open-ended questions that require the survey taker to provide a written response to a question, answers to focus group questions, and interview responses all fall into the category of qualitative information. Comments, suggestions, and reflections are the kinds of responses, both verbal and written, that will assist you in determining the success of your program.

Quantitative information is basically gathering and analyzing numbers. For example, how many people attended a workshop? On a scale of 1 to 5, how many participants rated the workshop a 5? If your program involved teaching a person a specific skill, could you evaluate his or her skill level before and after instruction? For example, giving someone a test to obtain her reading level by educational grade (i.e., grade 1, 2, 3 . . .) would be followed by literacy instruction. The individual would then be retested to see if her level of reading improved, did not improve, or stayed the same. The scores on both tests—along with the number of people who improved, did not improve, or stayed the same—would be considered quantitative information.

There are numerous sources, both online and in print, that further describe the evaluation process. Refer to these sources for additional information. As always, if you require further assistance, check with your local library.

AGREEMENTS

When reading through the grant information and application with attention to detail, take note of what you and your organization are agreeing to do once you accept the grant award. Government agencies frequently require that you submit progress reports and a final report upon completion of the project. Failure to meet these requirements might result in jeopardizing the awarding of any future grant. Foundations tend to be a bit more flexible in regard to reporting requirements. Nonetheless, communicating what you accomplished through the financial support you received and the impact that the activities had on your target population needs to be shared, in writing, with funders. It is important to maintain good relationships with those who are supporting your endeavors financially, as you may be in a position to request additional funding from them in the future.

SELECT A GRANT AND START WRITING!

Completing a grant application is no different from any other type of writing. It may take several rewrites, knowledgeable people to provide you with honest feedback, and a lot of patience to finish the final product. However, this should not discourage you. Once you begin answering questions on the application, your entire project should solidify quite easily.

If you have created your organization's grant toolkit (see chapter 2), answering the basic questions about your institution should be fairly easy. Unfortunately, if you do not have this information readily available, it might take you some time to gather and review it for accuracy.

REVIEW PROCESS

You will find that the process for deciding who receives full funding, partial funding, or no funding at all varies from grant funder to grant funder. Most government grants have very specific rules for how each grant application is to be rated. Depending upon the government agency, a grant application may follow this process:

1. Once received, your organization's contact information is separated from your grant application and a number is assigned to your proposal. Assigning a number ensures that reviewers are not aware of the organization submitting the proposal. Known as a "blind review," this process alleviates any favoritism that might occur if reviewers knew the grant applicant personally.
2. Three or more reviewers are provided copies of your application.
3. Each reviewer uses the same method to evaluate your project. This could be a page that allows the reviewer to assign points per pre-identified categories.
4. Reviewers "score" the application and might add written comments and suggestions.
5. The reviewers compare scores. Those applications that receive a wide range of scores are discussed. Reviewers do not need to have 100 percent consensus, but reasons why an application received a wide range of scores needs to be talked about to make sure that a reviewer did not miss or misread anything in the application.
6. Once the evaluation is complete, the reviewers' scores and comments are returned to the funding agency, where they are placed in rank order by score.
7. The agency uses a method of ranking applications further to determine funding, if necessary. On the top of the pile are fully funded projects, followed by partially funded, then projects not to receive funding.
8. The granting agency contacts the applicant, usually by regular mail, regarding the status of his or her grant proposal. Depending upon the agency, you also receive the reviewers' scoring as well as their notes and comments about your application. As is standard in the blind review process, you will not know who reviewed your application.

Government agencies with grant opportunities will post the deadline date for receiving applications, as well as the date by which grant awards will be announced. Award announcements will include the organizations that received the grants, how much money was awarded, as well as the titles of the projects. Brief descriptions of the projects may also be included.

The following is an example of a reviewer's evaluation sheet.

Example of a Reviewer's Grant Evaluation Sheet

Grant application number:

Title of grant:

Date grant submitted:

Date grant reviewed:

Numbers of grant reviewers:

Score:

Decision: fully fund　　　　partially fund　　　　do not fund

Table 6.5.　Sample Grant Evaluation Sheet

Maximum # of Points to Be Awarded Awarded	Category	Points
10	Application follows guidelines.	
10	Purpose of the grant is clear and easily understandable.	
10	Project timeline is realistic.	
10	Project budget is reasonable.	
10	Project meets grant criteria.	
50	Total:	
Comments:		

FROM A REVIEWER'S POINT OF VIEW

Reviewing grant applications can be a rewarding yet also a frustrating experience. Reading about various projects and their potential positive impact on society is a great learning experience. Such joy is quickly dampened when over one-half of the thirty or so grants you are reviewing are missing information, have major grammatical, typographical, and mathematical errors, or simply do not follow grant guidelines. These issues are big time wasters for a reviewer, and applications that fall within these categories do not bode well for being funded.

Common mistakes to avoid when preparing your grant application include:

1. Poor presentation of the application, including run-on sentences, typos, use of different fonts, use of line- and text-spacing variations, inconsistent use of margins, and similar treatments.
2. Inaccurate calculations; budget figures that do not reconcile with the budget narrative, for example.

3. Exceeding the number of pages allowed for the application.
4. Including extraneous or additional information, especially in terms of appendices.
5. Failure to answer the specific questions posed in the grant application.
6. Misnumbering of pages or not numbering the pages at all.
7. Including value judgments or specific political points of view.

Although these items may seem minor, they become glaring errors, especially when the grant application process is so highly competitive. You want to make sure that your application follows the grant guidelines to a "t."

TIPS FOR WRITING SUCCESSFUL GRANT APPLICATIONS

The following writing tips have proven very effective in procuring grant funding:

1. Write concisely and clearly. The goal is to communicate your need in the least number of words possible in order to keep the reviewer's time to a minimum. Most grant reviewers are not paid to read and recommend grants for funding, but do this on their own time. It is not good practice to write pages and pages of text. Such an approach usually ends up reading like you are begging the funders for money rather than demonstrating explicit need and the positive impact funding will have on the target audience.
2. Support your request with data and documentation. Grant guidelines will often state the amount of supporting material (usually in terms of paragraphs or pages) that is acceptable.
3. Provide meaningful data. Including data that is understandable and that directly applies to your request for funding is a plus, as numbers, charts, comments, and so forth give the reader a broader picture of your request, as well as show that research was done in support of your application. Resist the temptation to drown your reader in data.
4. Use neutral language. Write in a straightforward manner and be as objective as possible. Reviewers are not interested in your political views or value judgments about a topic.
5. Have someone read through the grant. Selecting someone who has little knowledge of your project will give you a fresh perspective on how grant readers might respond to your proposal. They can tell you if they easily understand what you are asking for, or if they have difficulty in comprehending what you are saying.

6. *Proofread!* Relying solely on a spellchecker is not good practice. Nothing will demote your application to the bottom of the pile faster than misspellings and incorrect grammar. Textual mistakes are easily spotted, showing the reviewer that you did not take the time to carefully review your own document prior to submission.

Using More than One Writer

A frequently asked question is whether more than one person should write the grant proposal. Dividing the work might make the process go faster. Those with expertise in particular areas, such as budgeting or describing the project succinctly, may also assist in composing the request. However, people usually have different writing styles. Proposals, as with most writing, are easier to read and understand if they are written in one voice—meaning that it reads as if one person wrote the text. Having more than one individual work on the proposal may be useful, but then it is good practice to have an experienced editor revise the application to ensure that the text is written in a consistent manner from section to section.

Hiring a Grant Writer

Professional grant writers can be located via the Internet through various websites. You may also come across a professor or another professional who has successfully written and received grants. Working with an individual to create an effective grant proposal takes many hours on the part of the writer. The process involves gaining an understanding of your organization and your request for funding, then writing and revising several drafts of the proposal. Rarely will individuals who write grants do this gratis. According to the American Grant Writers' Association, it is considered unethical for a grant writer to accept a percentage of the grant award as payment or receive compensation on the condition that the grant is procured. Additionally, it is very rare to be able to use grant funds to pay someone this type of compensation. Funding would need to be provided by your organization.

Should you and your organization think that hiring a grant writer is the best course of action, do your homework. Research the writer's background. Ask how many grants he or she has written that are similar in type and scope to your project, how many grants were funded, and what level of funding was awarded (e.g., did the grant receive the full amount of funding asked, or partial funding?). Talk to references who have used the writer's services to obtain their level of satisfaction. When you are satisfied with answers to these questions, then be prepared to pay the individual, either by the hour or by contract. Have a signed contract with the individual that details what work is to be completed, as well as when payment will be made (e.g., pay 50 percent up front and 50 percent when the proposal is completed to your satisfaction).

Including Additional Information

As has been said throughout this text, reviewers do not have the time to read book-length grant applications. Guidelines often indicate the maximum number of pages of the proposal. Information might also be provided as to how many types of attachments can be added to the proposal, as well as what information can be appended. Sometimes you will be allowed to include visuals, such as photos, a concept design, or architectural blueprints. Additionally, the application may require that you include letters of support from individuals or agencies not affiliated with your organization. If this is a requirement, obtain permission from the person who would write the support letter well in advance of the application deadline in order to make sure that he or she will, in fact, support your request for funding. It also gives the individual plenty of time to write a cogent letter of support and send it to you before the deadline date.

A word of caution is necessary here. Grant guidelines are very specific and will frequently state the maximum length of the proposal, as well as what information can be included and what documentation should not be included. Do not provide this additional information if the guidelines prohibit it. Sometimes there is a tendency for grant writers to want to include as much information as possible in the hopes that this additional information will persuade the reviewers to fund the project. In reality, not following the guidelines tells the reviewers that you do not adhere to directions, which then might lead them to the conclusion that, if you are unable to follow instructions, how would you be able to successfully complete the grant if it were funded? I have also witnessed cases where grant reviewers were told not to read beyond the maximum number of pages, so any appended material was ignored. In other words, submitting more information than is required will not improve your odds of obtaining funding.

Once you are confident that you have followed the instructions for the grant application and that all the information provided is accurate, it is time to submit your proposal. Submitting your proposal is the topic of chapter 7.

CONCLUSION

Completing a grant proposal takes time, energy, effort, and patience. This chapter provided you with practical advice and suggestions on how to create a fundable grant application. Adhering to grant guidelines, understanding what your organization is agreeing to upon accepting the grant award, and taking grant-writing tips into consideration will go a long way toward producing a fundable proposal. Knowing the pitfalls in using more than one writer to compose the application or hiring a grant writer will save you time and work, too. Submitting the correct information as indicated by the granting agency will make your grant more noticeable over other submissions.

7

Submitting Your Grant

Submitting your grant is probably the second-largest event in the life cycle of the grant process, with the first being receiving the grant itself! Although grant submission is fairly easy and uneventful, there are a few tips that will help you make the process go smoothly and without incident.

WORDS OF ADVICE

Before you hit that button to send your grant application over the Web or before you drop your package in the mailbox, there are a few tasks that, if completed, will save you a lot of time and headache down the road.

1. After you have read the application over and had a few others review the information for accuracy, including that the text is error free, read it over one more time! That final check will ensure that you have included all the documentation required and that it is in the proper order. You would be amazed at what is missed or needs correction during this final check. Remember that you only have one opportunity to persuade the reviewers to fund your project and you need to make sure that you have done everything possible to submit the best grant application that you can.

2. Make a copy of the complete grant application package for yourself. Whether this is a print copy or electronic version that is backed up in some manner, this is a critical step that is often overlooked. People tend to save the grant documentation in various places, such as having a copy of the main text in one location, the appendices in another

place, and the budget still somewhere else. It will save you a tremendous amount of time in the future if you keep a master copy of everything you submitted, together, just as you submitted it.

3. Submit your application a few days in advance of the deadline date. If the Internet is down or the software used to enter grant documentation is not working properly, you will have a few days to work through this issue prior to the deadline date. And if, for some reason, regular mail is delayed, your package should still arrive on time.

4. Use a return-receipt-requested feature if at all possible, which gives you the paperwork to show that you did, in fact, send the package prior to the deadline date. Asking the agency or foundation to sign for your package is usually not done, as it places a burden on the funder to have someone present to accept and sign for your grant submission. Most electronic submission systems will send you a return e-mail message that your application has been successfully submitted. The point here is to make sure that you have some type of receipt, either paper or electronic, as proof that the grant was submitted on time.

5. Wait and be patient! It is rare that you will hear whether or not your grant has been funded within a week or two of submission. Reviewers may meet once a month, once a quarter, or only once a year. Most government agencies and foundations will have provided you with a date when grants will be announced. It is not good form to pester the grant-giving organization by asking when grants will be awarded. You just need to be patient. Submit the grant and forget about it.

SAME GRANT, DIFFERENT FUNDERS

Many times the question is posed as to whether or not you should submit the same grant to more than one government agency or foundation. Most times, the answer is "no." Those who might award you money may decide that the other potential funder will support your project and thus will not fund your specific grant. This would essentially null your chances of obtaining monies from two or more institutions.

It may be possible, however, to simultaneously submit your proposal to more than one funding source if you indicate up front that you are doing so. As long as the grant guidelines do not preclude you from simultaneous grant submissions, and as long as you are transparent with the agency or foundation that this is your plan of action, this should not be problematic. If you have already procured funding from one or more different sources, then absolutely include this information in your application, describing this in text, as well as including this information in your budget. Make sure that you state whether or not (a) you have the funding in hand; (b) you have been awarded the funding and are waiting for it to arrive; or (c) you are going to ask for funding in the hopes that you will be given the award. Frequently, funding organizations see multiple sources of financing a project in a positive way, as it indicates your organization's willingness to collaborate with other entities.

Seeking and procuring grant funds from multiple sources is good fiscal management. Collaborations of this kind strengthen your organization's position in the community. It demonstrates to others the flexibility and openness you have to work toward a common purpose. Overall, it is a good thing. Caution just needs to be heeded in following grant guidelines and regulations.

SITE VISITS

If you submit a grant that requests a large sum of money (such as $1 million or more) and that covers several years, the government agency or foundation may request a site visit. A site visit can be requested at any time—before the grant is approved, during the grant, and after the grant has ended. The granting organization may send one individual or an entire team of people. However the site visit manifests itself, you need to be ultra-prepared to persuade site visitors why you need the funding and to answer all of their questions and concerns.

Preparing for a site visit is like preparing to host a premier event. Everything—from building appearance to documentation—must be in top-notch condition. Mistakes, errors, and missteps will be remembered. Handling these types of visits requires a detail-oriented individual who possesses a people personality. Here are several recommendations when preparing and conducting a site visit:

- Involve your entire staff. Share all specifics that you have about the visit and allow staff members to assist you in planning. Impress upon them the need to be professional and courteous. Appearances are everything, so a good cleaning and organization of office and other work spaces is in order. Messy areas will give visitors the impression that your organization is disorganized, leading them to believe that you might be just as disorganized with their funding.
- Educate and remind your staff about the elements of the project, the history of your organization, and the names of board members and project participants. Provide your staff with a few key talking points of why the organization needs funding. Frequently, site visitors will ask these types of questions of staff and you want them to be prepared.
- If your organization resides within a building where there is a reception area or a security process, inform the receptionist and security about

the visit, including the names, titles, and other contact information of who will be attending, as well as the dates and times of arrivals and departures. Clarify parking requirements if there are any. Share all of this information with your guests.

- Unless you will be organizing and conducting the site visit yourself, appoint one employee (preferably a full-time employee) to be the point person for the visit. This individual will communicate with the site visit team on such items as date, time, and location confirmation; arrange for travel, lodging, and meal requests (if appropriate); serve as the conduit for sending and receiving information such as agendas, notes, and supporting material; and make and confirm meal arrangements, catering, and the like. Having only one person doing these tasks will greatly reduce the possibility of miscommunications.
- As executive director of your organization, work with the visitors to develop a mutually agreed-upon agenda of activities (What do they want to see? Who would they like to talk to?). Ask them what type of documentation they would like to review and whether they want this information in advance of their visit.
- Prepare yourself. Be able to speak intelligently and clearly about your proposal, especially including how funding will make a positive impact on the target audience you serve. As Karsh and Fox (2003) recommend, be enthusiastic about your work and about the organization. Visitors look for commitment, energy, enthusiasm, and the capacity to implement the proposed program successfully. This is no time to be reticent and shy about explaining who you are and what you do.
- Be the ultimate host. Have refreshments and snacks available at all meetings. Ask if anyone has specific dietary restrictions. Offer to transport them to and from the airport or train station to your organization and their hotel. Nothing is more off-putting than going to a new location and having to figure out your own way around. If the site visit will be over several days, ask visitors to join you for dinner and ask if there are any areas of interest in your city that they would like to see.
- There is no need to provide gifts. Sometimes gift giving is prohibited. However, providing a packet of information about your organization and the surrounding communities is always appreciated, as is providing some food (fruit, chocolate, etc.) in the visitors' hotel room. They may have had a very long trip getting to your city and may not have had time to eat. The provision of small snacks with a welcome card is a nice touch that will be remembered.
- Several days after the visit, send a letter to each guest, thanking him or her for visiting your organization and letting each one know that you are available to answer any questions he or she may have.

Your goal is to make their visit as easy and pleasant as possible. Two items that people always seem to remember are the quality of the food and the level of comfort (Was the room too hot, too cold? etc.). Maximizing the visitor's experience will go a long way during and after the visit itself.

CONCLUSION

Finally sending a completed grant proposal to a potential funder is a milestone when seeking financial support. You'll experience a big sigh of relief once the information leaves your office. Taking the time to do a last check of the documentation, making a complete copy for yourself, and sending in the application several days in advance of the deadline date will alleviate or lessen any problems that may arise. Simultaneously submitting the same grant application to multiple government agencies or foundations is traditionally not done. However, if the guidelines do not prohibit simultaneous submissions, having multiple sources of funding might, in fact, strengthen your proposal. If a site visit is part of the funding process, be prepared. You, your staff, board members, and grant participants need to persuade the site visitors of the need for funding.

8

Making the Grant Successful

Receiving word that your proposal will be funded is one of the greatest feelings in the world! It is validation by someone else that your project is worth implementation, so much so that the funders are willing to provide your organization with money to make your project happen. When you receive this exciting news, celebrate! Tell everyone! Share the award announcement, because after the good news is known, the time for more hard work begins. This chapter guides you through the time period immediately after you accept the award to when your project is completed.

GETTING TO WORK

You've received the award. You've celebrated. Now it is time to get down to work. The key here is: Do not wait to start! The sooner you start implementing your grant-funded project, the better you will be in the long run. You will be amazed at how quickly time flies when you are working on a grant-funded project. Grant timelines can be brief, ranging anywhere from a few months to a few years. Unless funding is renewed for longer periods of time, a grant starts and ends within a specific span of time. Almost like writing a paper, you do not want to wait until the last minute to begin.

READ REQUIREMENTS CAREFULLY

A significant amount of time may have passed between the time you submitted your application and the time you are awarded funding. Chances are you may have forgotten all the details involved in your project, so a good first step is to read through the original proposal. Carefully take note of the timeline of activities. Transferring the timeline to a large wall calendar or electronic calendar where you can view it every day serves as a terrific visual reminder of where you are in the process and will assist you in meeting project deadlines.

If you are required to submit progress reports, as well as a final report to the funders, make note of this on your calendar. Missing a deadline can be detrimental to receiving all of the promised grant funding (if you did not receive all of the monies up front) as well as possibly jeopardizing future grant opportunities. Should anything prevent you from meeting stated guidelines, inform the grant funders immediately so that the timeline can be adjusted.

A WORD ABOUT COMPLIANCE

This book focuses on searching and writing nonscientific grants—grants that do not involve experiments or human or animal subjects. Federal funding programs available through such agencies as the National Institutes of Health (NIH) or the National Science Foundation (NSF) have strict regulations related to issues of compliance. These regulations dictate every item related to a grant program—from accounting procedures to administrative requirements. Being in compliance with these regulations is required when you receive a federal grant award directly, when the funding comes from the federal government via another agency (such as a state library), or when the Office of Management and Budget (OMB) circulars specifically indicate that the requirements are applicable. Federal government rules are applicable to federal funding whether or not a project involves experiments, or human or animal subjects.

Moreover, many educational institutions (pre-K through postdoctoral programs) and other nonprofits may require adherence to the federal guidelines even if your grant is not from a federally funded agency. What follows is a very brief introduction to some of the more commonly referred to federal government regulations regarding grant funding.

The Office of Management and Budget (OMB) resides in the Executive Office of the U.S. president. Its mission is "to assist the President in overseeing the preparation of the federal budget and to supervise its administration in Executive Branch agencies" (http://www.whitehouse.gov/omb/, accessed 22 February 2010). The OMB issues instructions or other relevant information to federal agencies through "circulars" and "bulletins." The purpose of a circular is to communicate instructions and information on topics considered continuous or ongoing. Bulletins address one-time actions. Circulars and bulletins were established under revised Circular No. A-1. For more information, see http://www.whitehouse.gov/omb/circulars_a001/.

Three circulars that may be relevant to your grant writing are:

- *Circular A-21: Cost Principles for Educational Institutions* (also referenced as 2 CFR Parts 215 and 220, where CFR refers to the Code of Federal Regulations) provides guidelines and explanations for what can be considered total allowable direct costs for federally funded grants. Circular A-21 will tell you what items you can pay out of your budget and what items are not allowed. Such categories as "reasonable costs," "allocable costs," and "limitations on allowance of costs" are defined. For example, the following are expressly unallowable for direct costs under Circular A-21: alcoholic beverages, alumni activities, lobbying, automobile for personal use, housing and personal living expenses, and so on. Other costs listed as not allowable with exceptions include pre-agreement costs, fees related to changes in travel, and student activity costs. These are just some examples of the types of requirements provided in Circular A-21.

- *Circular A-110: Uniform Administrative Requirements for Grants and Other Agreements with Institutions of Higher Education, Hospitals, and Other Non-Profit Organizations* provides administrative requirements for sponsored awards. Common terms such as "award," "cost-share," and "subrecipient" are defined. Pre-award, post-award, and closeout process requirements are also described.

- *Circular A-133: Audits of States, Local Governments, and Non-Profit Organizations* provides the responsibilities of external auditors as well as administrative requirements of federal awards that must be followed. The goal of Circular A-133 is to gain consistency and uniformity among federal agencies for auditing nonfederal groups (such as educational institutions, and state and local governments) that receive and expend federal awards.

COMMON COMPLIANCE ISSUES AND IMPACTS

Here are some of the more frequent errors made when managing a grant program that must comply with OMB regulations:

- Charging unallowable costs directly to the grant.
- Payment for items, services, and activities that fall outside the grant's official timeline.
- Failure to review financial accounts on a monthly basis.
- Failure to provide supporting documentation.

What happens if you fail to comply with federal government requirements? There are several repercussions that can occur if you do not follow the prescribed guidelines:

- Fines or sanctions may be applied by the federal government.
- Your organization may be required to repay funds to the sponsoring agency.
- Your organization may be opened up to additional external audits.
- You might be placing future funding opportunities in jeopardy.
- You will damage your reputation and that of the institution or organization you work for.

Saint Louis University's director of sponsored programs, Joseph Sanning, provides the following advice for being successful in the area of federal grant compliance:

- Make sure that all costs are allowable per grant requirements and charged to the grant funds within the official time frame of the grant.
- Review budget and costs in a timely manner. Monthly reviews are recommended.
- If you need to do cost transfers, make sure they are both timely and allowable.
- Document all costs. Documentation should always indicate that the charge is allowable under the grant.

If you fail to do cost transfers within sixty days, your documentation should address the "Five Ws"—Who, What, When, Where, and Why—as well as an explanation of what procedures will be implemented so that this delay does not reoccur.

Being in compliance with federal government rules and regulations is critical on many levels. Knowing what items and services you can and cannot charge to your grant, managing your budget closely and accurately, and keeping current with any changes to the regulations is imperative to successfully completing your grant project. Failing to comply can result in serious consequences, including paying back a portion or all of the grant funds, paying additional fines, not being able to receive grant funding in the future, and damaging your reputation and that of your organization.

ORDERING AND HIRING

Time goes by very quickly on grant projects. Staying on top of the work that needs to be accomplished is important to making sure that your grant project is successful. In this regard, there are two tasks that should be started immediately after you receive the grant.

First, if you need to order equipment, supplies, software, or other products, do so as soon as possible. Software, hardware, other types of equipment, and specialized supplies can be out of stock, placed on backorder, or discontinued. As well, you may need to create and announce a Request for Information (RFI) or Request for Proposal (RFP) to obtain three or more quotes for a specific part of your project. Usually this occurs when the cost is over a specified amount (such as $5,000) or is a requirement of the granting agency or foundation. Purchasing all the materials that you need, as well as working through the bidding process, can take months. The best advice is to use time to your advantage by beginning these tasks early on in the grant cycle.

Second, if you need to hire staff, contract with a consultant, or outsource specific services, post advertisements immediately and in multiple locations. Make your job announcements available on your website, through professional associations, on electronic mailing lists, blogs, in online newspapers, and so on. If the job you are hiring for is short term (e.g., less than twelve to fifteen months), focus your advertising locally and regionally. Chances are that someone from outside your immediate commuting area will not apply or accept a position that is only for a few months. There are exceptions, but most positions of this type are filled from within and around surrounding communities.

Depending upon your type of library or organization, you may be required to follow specific Affirmative Action, Equal Employment Opportunity, immigration, or other diversity requirements. Be watchful that you follow legal hiring and other personnel regulations. You may put your grant-funded project in jeopardy if these regulations are not followed. If you are unsure if your library or organization needs to adhere to such regulations or if you need guidance in this area, check with your local area employment office or read available information online.

RECOGNIZING THOSE WHO SUPPORT YOU

Formally recognizing the government agencies, foundations, and individuals that are financially supporting your project may not be a requirement, but it is considered an important part of accepting funding. Simple public recognition is always greatly appreciated. You do not need to do a large fancy reception. Sometimes a formal check presentation or grand opening is appropriate. It depends on your project, the level of funding, the grant requirements, and the expectations of the funding agency, foundation, or individual.

Sending out press releases when you receive the grant and when your project ends is a good idea. If your project is large enough, you can announce major milestones along the way. Before submitting press releases to media outlets, make sure that the funders are in agreement with this. Sometimes the funding organization will want to write its own press release. Sometimes they will agree that you should write the press release as long as they have the opportunity to review the release prior to its submission to the media. When in doubt, always double-check with the funders.

Another way funders may require you to acknowledge their support is by providing a statement on any material related to your project that is made public. Let's say you received funding from the American Cancer Society to host a benefit run. ACS might require you to print text on your project-related information, such as websites, flyers, and t-shirts, that says something like "This event is being supported in part by the American Cancer Society." This gives the funding organization public acknowledgment and also lets the community know that the organization is financially supporting your event.

Public recognition can be quite beneficial. For the funding organization, it sends the message that their institution is supportive of a specific mission. For your library or nonprofit organization, it demonstrates your willingness to partner with others to make something happen that is beneficial to society. In both cases, it is a good and very inexpensive—or, almost always, a free—source of publicity and name recognition.

When openly acknowledging support from funders, make sure that it is done with grace, that it is well planned, and that there is no chance of embarrassing those involved with your project. The last thing you would want to happen is for your funders to either pull their financial support or not fund you again because you made a gaffe or error at their expense.

CONCLUSION

The purpose of this chapter is to provide you with advice that has proven to be successful in the grant world. Knowing all the components of your project and being quite familiar with your timeline of activities is imperative. Ordering equipment early and advertising for staff immediately upon receiving the grant award will go a long way in implementing your project successfully. Formally recognizing the agency, foundation, or individual that is supporting you engenders good will. Being attentive to these seemingly small but important details will greatly assist you in achieving your project goals.

9

Some Advice and Final Words

This book is intended to guide you through the grant process. From gathering background information on your library or organization to selecting a fundable project, from identifying possible sources of funding to writing and submitting the application, and from accepting the grant award to formally recognizing the funders, it is hoped that you have gained an understanding of the workings of the grant-writing process.

KEEPING YOUR SANITY

As you read this text, the thought may have crossed your mind that the grant research and writing process is most often straightforward and somewhat formulaic. This is true, to a point. But if you fully engage yourself and others in the endeavor of seeking funding, you might find times when you and your team experience unexpected challenges. Writer's block may stop you in your tracks for a time. Thinking that your idea is not innovative or creative enough to warrant funding might emerge. Grant guidelines may change, your application may become lost, or the data you analyze may not support your proposed project. Of course, such roadblocks appear just to make the grant procurement process all that more adventurous!

WORDS FROM EXPERIENCE

The following story is a good example of being flexible so that the grant proposal moves ahead. A group of nonprofits, government agencies, and libraries in a particular region was interested in collaborating on a multi-agency project. Each participating entity owned a collection of archival items of historical significance to the region. The collections included diaries, photographs, VHS videotapes, Civil War records, books, and other related print materials. The goal was to establish a regional repository of materials, bringing items housed in disparate locations together under one roof. Operational expenses, such as personnel, technologies, storage, cataloging, and description, would be shared financially by all, making this a cost-effective, one-stop shop for items of regional historical value.

Sounds like a super plan—different organizations with similar missions working together for the betterment of the community. A planning outline was written with input from all interested participants. Grant funding was identified to support construction and renovation of a building, as well as to financially support the operation for the first year. For the first two months of this endeavor, everything seemed to be on target.

The third month of the project involved developing a more specific plan connected to the grant-funding guidelines. Extensive conversations were held with the entire group, as well as individually with each participating organization. What began to emerge were issues and concerns not voiced in previous conversations: Who would be held ultimately responsible if items in the shared storage facility were damaged or stolen? Since the collections are of different sizes, shouldn't the groups with larger collections pay more than those with smaller collections? What if the less financially affluent organizations are small but have large collections?

These conversations continued through the third month, the fourth month, and into the fifth month. At this point, with the deadline for grant applications only eight weeks away, consensus had not been reached on these and other important concerns. Additionally, it was discovered that one organization was insisting (outside of face-to-face group discussions) that the storage facility be connected to their home base—a mansion in the process of being restored—and that additional funding was required to complete that project. It was perceived that this particular organization had a definite self-interest in wanting to be a part of the collaborative effort. A member of another organization held most of the group's collection in his home and was resisting turning over "his" collection to the storage facility. Other groups had personnel changes, so that the founding grant group was experiencing turnover.

With only four weeks to go to the grant deadline, the final proposal looked significantly different from the first vision of the project. A few organizations dropped out of the project for various reasons (not enough personnel to dedicate to the process or project implementation, resistance to participating in a shared storage facility, fear and trepidation of the unknown in attempting something new, etc.). In the end, what was originally conceived as a physical shared storage facility with shared resources and personnel turned out to be a much smaller project. The final grant application requested funding to (a) hire an archivist to conduct a preliminary assessment of each collection, (b) select and implement a shared online catalog, and (c) develop a plan to complete inventorying, cataloging, and describing the items in each participating group's collection. The grant was submitted on time and the project was fully funded. Clearly, this story is an example of starting with a well-intentioned idea of improving storage of and access to important historical assets and ending with achieving a portion of that goal.

GAINING INSIGHT FROM A REVIEWER

The task of reviewing grant applications is also frequently fraught with challenges as well as disappointments, in addition to a sense of accomplishment. Most reviewers volunteer their time to read through grant proposals, most of which are the size of a small book. This service is taken very seriously. As such, a reviewer will block out hours of time to read and reread each proposal, comparing the application to the grant guidelines. Sometimes reviewers are required to rank the proposals in terms of fully fund, partially fund, and not fund. At the final stage, reviewers who have read the same proposals discuss their findings and recommendations.

By being a reviewer, you gain quite a bit of knowledge. You read about interesting and innovative projects usually involving nontraditional collaborations or implementation of the latest technologies, instructional techniques, service operations, and so on. If you review grants from a wide geographical area—the United States, for example—you begin to appreciate the diverse nature of our country, as well as the similarities and differences in the challenges each community faces.

A reviewer might be responsible for reading and ranking a few proposals to looking over 100 or so applications. In serving as a reviewer, being thorough in a timely manner is of the utmost importance. So why would a seemingly enjoyable experience become aggravating and frustrating? The answer to this question is fairly easy.

As a reviewer, you schedule blocks of time in your calendar (including nights and weekends) to provide this service to the granting organization. There is no average set time that one allocates to read through one proposal. At the outset, a review may take fifteen minutes or it may take more than an hour. So, you are a reviewer who has settled into a comfortable place, coffee or other favorite beverage in hand, along with your favorite writing instrument. Your goal is to do an initial read through each proposal over the next several hours.

The first few applications pique your interest. Each is well written, following the application guidelines. Proposed projects are creative and indicate positive impacts on target populations. Budget items are allowable, with suggested costs in acceptable ranges. So far, so good.

Reviewing begins to get bumpy about the sixth application. Application six is written concisely but does not follow grant guidelines. Pages are not numbered and the content included is out of sequence. You spend extra time attempting to match the application with the grant guidelines. This proves to be frustrating and with so many more grants to review, many of which probably follow the guidelines exactly, you set this one aside and continue to application seven.

The content of this application includes less than the minimal explanations, justifications, and data required for consideration. Cover sheet data is accurate, but the remaining application is incomplete—several sections are not answered, the budget figures are actually ranges of costs, and a budget narrative is not included—leading the reviewer to question why anyone would take the time to submit such a poor package. This application is set in the "do not fund" pile.

Various egregious as well as less egregious errors appear as you move through the remainder of the applications. Here and there are misspelled words or an inaccurately placed decimal point. These errors, albeit unfortunate, may not be enough to discard the application, so they are placed in the "to re-review" pile. A few more applications are as badly written or incomplete as application number seven. These are automatically placed in the "do not fund" pile. After four hours, you complete the first review of forty applications and have placed ten in the "do not fund" pile, five in the "definitely fund" pile, and the remainder in the "re-review" pile.

You will repeat this process another day by intensely reviewing the "re-review" pile of applications. On this day, you might find additional errors. You will try to match the proposals that are somewhat out of order with the grant guidelines. However, if this exercise goes to a level of frustration, these applications will be placed in a new pile—"probably do not fund."

The point of this anecdote is to illustrate that reviewing is a challenging yet rewarding exercise. Even knowing that the process is time consuming, reviewers take this work very seriously, wanting to be confident that each application is given its due with a careful review and recommendation for funding.

WHAT IF WE DO NOT GET THE GRANT?

One question that remains unanswered is: What happens if you do not receive the grant? More often than not, you will receive rejection letters.

Even when you believe that you have done everything possible to make your grant application the best that it can be, it may not be fully funded or partially funded. This result could have nothing to do with your grant application itself but may have everything to do with the increased competition for scarce resources.

If you are not successful with obtaining funding, take a step back and regroup. Request to read the reviewers notes about your proposal. Usually anonymous, reviewers' notes will provide you with insight as to what the readers believed were the strengths and weaknesses of your project. Frequently, more than one reviewer is assigned to read grant applications, so you will be able to read more than one person's opinion. There may or may not be official reviewer notes recorded for you to read. It depends on the funding organization and its process for selecting projects to fund.

Another approach is to talk to your contact at the agency or foundation. With this conversation, you might be able to determine if your proposal completely missed the mark as to what the grant funders were looking for to support financially. Or you may discover that your application is salvageable and, with more work, the agency or foundation may be open to having you resubmit your project in the future.

Being rejected for grant funds is disappointing. You and your team have probably spent many hours researching, writing, rewriting, and double-checking to create a persuasive proposal. Prior to submitting the application to another funding source or resubmitting to the same organization but addressing their questions, assess whether or not you want to edit your proposal or if you want to try and submit your request to another source for funding.

MAINTAIN PERSPECTIVE

Remember that a lot of time has passed between submitting the grant application and receiving word that you did or did not receive funding. During this time, things might have changed. People come and go; financial realities shift; an event may have happened that makes your project no longer viable. Organizational needs may have changed, so you may find yourself in a position of having to turn down grant funding. If this occurs, be gracious and forthcoming. Apprise the funders of your current situation; indicate why you are not able to accept the award at this time. If appropriate and if it will work for your organization, ask whether the start of the grant can be delayed. Declining a grant is not a bad thing. It happens. The best advice here is to convey to the funders that, although you are unable to accept monies at this time, you would still like to maintain good relations, with the possibility that you might apply for funding in the future.

CONCLUSION

Grant writing is a time-consuming, intellectually challenging, and very rewarding experience. Receiving financial funding from another entity validates the work of your organization. Even if you do not obtain funding, you and your organization will have gained invaluable experience working through all aspects of the granting process.

Completing applications requires knowledge of your organization's mission and vision; a thorough understanding of what the organization can and cannot do in terms of accepting funds; and the ability to translate your ideas into language that moves others to provide monies so that you are able to accomplish your goals. This text is to guide you through what seems to many as a very difficult maze. I hope that you will refer to this book over and over again as you seek funding by writing successful grants.

Appendix A: Samples of a Three-Year Strategic Plan Outline

SAMPLE 1: THREE-YEAR STRATEGIC PLAN OUTLINE FOR LITERACY VOLUNTEERS, INC.

Literacy Volunteers, Inc. (LVI) was established in 1910 with the mission of teaching volunteers throughout the United States how to teach children and adults basic reading skills. For over ninety years, LVI has partnered with local area public libraries and other community groups to establish literacy volunteers in their own communities. Starting in 1910 with a budget of $50, financial support for this nonprofit organization has grown to $10 million. This strategic plan, created with input from board members and volunteers, provides goals and objectives LVI will accomplish in the next three years. See table A.1.

SAMPLE 2: THREE-YEAR STRATEGIC PLAN OUTLINE FOR EQUINES FOR OTHERS, INC.

Equines for Others, Inc. (EFO) began in 1989 as a small, all-volunteer operation with the goal of providing equine-assisted therapy for physically and mentally challenged children, ages seven to sixteen, using rescued horses. Over the past decade, EFO has established itself as a reputable and safe facility serving more than 350 children with a permanent staff of four and fifty-five volunteers. This strategic plan, developed by the EFO community, sets forth the goals to be accomplished or exceeded over the next three years. Timing of action items is funding dependent. See table A.2.

Table A.1

Year One		
Goal Statements	*Action Steps and Timeline*	*Performance Measures*
Goal 1: Make LVI programming as widely available as possible throughout the United States. Objective 1: Expand LVI programs to rural areas.	1st month: Identify rural locations. 2nd month: Conduct a needs assessment and environmental scan. 6th month: Develop budget for expansion.	By x month: List of rural locations identified and reviewed for potential expansion. By x month: Needs assessment (survey and focus group) and environmental scan completed in selected rural areas. By x month: Budget with estimated figures completed.
Goal 2: Make LVI better known. Objective 2: Update website.	1st month: Hire Web designer. Budget $5,000 from General Fund. 6th month: Launch new website.	By x month: New website will be up and running. Number of unique hits on the new website will increase by 25% over old website.

Year Two		
Goal 1: Make LVI programming as widely available as possible throughout the United States. Objective 1: Expand LVI programs into rural areas.	1st month: Identify two rural locations within close proximity of each other. Search for and select grant funding opportunity. 2nd month: Write and submit grant. 6th month: If grant received, implement project. If not, seek alternative funding.	By x month: Two rural locations will be identified with contacts confirmed in both communities to be part of the project By x month: Grant received. Implement project immediately OR Grant not received and look for alternative funding.

Year Three		
Goal 1: Make LVI programming as widely available as possible throughout the United States. Objective 1: Expand LVI programs into rural areas.	Entire year: Implement grant project. Follow project timeline, budget, and implementation schedule.	By x month: Project completed. Survey offered and results analyzed. At least 50% of respondents will indicate project helped them learn how to teach others how to read.

Table A.2.

Overall Goal: Build a permanent equestrian facility within three years to better serve the growing client base.

Year One:

    Action Steps:

        Develop a capital fund-raising campaign with the goal of raising $1 million by year three.

        Hire an architectural firm with equestrian facility construction experience.

        Hold community forum for input on the design of the new facility.

    Performance Measures:

        Capital fund-raising campaign committee established and campaign started in year one.

        Architectural firm selected through bidding process. Concept plan created by the end of year one.

        Community forum held immediately after concept plan is available.

Year Two:

    Action Steps:

        Continue with capital fund-raising campaign.

        Finalize concept plan.

        Share concept plan with broader community for final feedback.

    Performance Measures:

        Capital fund-raising campaign reaches 50 percent of its goal.

        Concept plan is finalized.

        Second open forum for community input is completed.

Year Three:

    Action Steps:

        Wrap up capital fund-raising campaign.

        Break ground on new equestrian facility.

    Performance Measures:

        Capital fund-raising campaign meets or exceeds the $1 million target.

        Official ground-breaking ceremony is held by the end of year three.

            Facility to be completed within twelve months of breaking ground.

Appendix B: Sample Entries for Government Grants

SAMPLE 1

This sample was modified from http://www.grants.gov (accessed 22 February 2010).

Child Care Access Mean Parents in School (CCAMPIS) Program
CFDA 84.335A

Document Type:	Grants Notice
Funding Opportunity Number:	ED-GRANTS-040809–001
Opportunity Category:	Discretionary
Posted Date:	April 08, 2009
Creation Date:	April 08, 2009
Funding Instrument Type:	Grant
Category of Funding Activity:	Education
Expected Number of Awards:	119
Estimated Total Program Funding:	$10,714,000
Award Ceiling:	$300,000
Award Floor:	$10,000
Cost Sharing or Matching Requirement:	No

Eligible Applicants:
> Public and state-controlled institutions of higher education.
> Private institutions of higher education.

Agency Name: Department of Education

Purpose of Program: The CCAMPIS Program supports the participation of low-income parents in postsecondary education through the provision of campus-based child care services. For specific information about eligibility, please see the official application notice. The official version of this document is the document published in the *Federal Register* at http://www.access.gpo.gov/NARA/index.html.

SAMPLE 2

This sample was modified from http://www.grants.gov (accessed 22 February 2010).
America's Historical and Cultural Organizations Planning Grants
CFDA 45.164
Document Type: Grants Notice
URL: http://www.neh.gov/grants/guidelines/AHCO_PlanningGuidelines.html
Opportunity Category: Discretionary
Posted Date: October 08, 2009
Creation Date: October 08, 2009
Funding Instrument Type: Grant
Category of Funding Activity: Humanities
Expected Number of Awards: 30
Award Ceiling: $75,000
Award Floor: $0
Cost Sharing or Matching Requirement: No
Eligible Applicants
    Public and state-controlled institutions of higher education.
    Native American tribal governments (federally recognized).
    Nonprofits having a 501(c)(3) status with the IRS, other than institutions of higher education.
    Private institutions of higher education.
Agency Name: National Endowment for the Humanities
Description: America's Historical and Cultural Organizations grants support projects in the humanities that explore stories, ideas, and beliefs that deepen our understanding of our lives and our world. NEH offers two categories of grants for America's Historical and Cultural Organizations: Planning Grants and Implementation Grants. Planning grants are available for projects that may need further development before applying for implementation. This planning can include the identification and refinement of the project's main humanities ideas and questions, consultation with scholars in order to strengthen the humanities content, preliminary audience evaluation, preliminary design of the proposed interpretive formats, beta testing of digital formats, development of complementary programming, research at archives or sites whose resources might be used, or the drafting

of interpretive materials. Applicants are not required to obtain a planning grant before applying for an implementation grant. Applicants may not, however, submit multiple applications for the same project at the same deadline. If an application for a project is already under review, another application for the same project cannot be accepted.

Appendix C: Sample Query Letter

[date]

Abigail Jones
Grant Administrator
ABC Foundation
400 Lexington Ave.
Washington, DC 20012

Dear Ms. Jones:

Our organization, Jamestown Literacy Volunteers (JLV), is submitting this query letter for consideration of our project, "Reading on the Road," as fundable under the ABC Foundation's "Enhancing Literacy" grant program. According to grant guidelines, it is our understanding that a query letter is required prior to submission of a grant application.

Established in 1989, JLV has twenty years of teaching adults in our community how to read. Our fifteen-member board includes certified reading specialists and public librarians with extensive experience implementing adult literacy programming. In partnership with the Jamestown Public Library, we have trained over fifteen volunteers how to teach adults, one-on-one, to obtain basic literacy skills. Our organization is interested in expanding its reach to the rural areas surrounding our community. Financial support is needed to bring literacy programming to the people who need it most.

Titled "Reading on the Road," our project will be led by Sarah Hunter, PhD, a local literacy expert. Over a period of six months, we plan on teaching basic reading skills to approximately 150 adults who reside in rural areas that surround our community.

Our research shows that 15 percent of adults living in rural areas in our region are illiterate. As a result, they are unable to perform daily functions such as writing a check or reading a newspaper. These individuals are apt to be unemployed. With your support, we will bring the necessary skill of reading to adults in the hopes that they will become functioning members of our community.

We anticipate that the total cost of this project will be $3,250. JLV has received confirmation that the Jamestown Public Library will be providing $250 toward this project. JVL will collaborate with your agency to market and promote this program. To this end, we are seeking a total of $3,000 from the "Enhancing Literacy" grant program.

Our organizations share the same mission—to teach others how to read so that an entire new world of opportunity and enjoyment can be opened up to them. This project fully supports our goal.

Thank you for taking the time to consider funding our "Reading on the Road" project. Together we will be able to change individuals' lives for the better. Please do not hesitate to contact me, Lynn Palmer, Executive Director, Jamestown Literacy Volunteers, at 716–333–1212 or e-mail lpalm@jlv.org

Warmest regards,

Lynn Palmer
Executive Director
Jamestown Literacy Volunteers

Jean Carpenter
Mayor, Jamestown, NY
and
President of the JVL Board of Directors

Appendix D: Sample Entries for Foundations

SAMPLE 1

This sample is modified from COS Funding Opportunities (accessed 22 February 2010).

COS Unique ID:	59197
Date Last Revised:	July 7, 2009, 12:00 AM
Title:	Grants for Libraries
Sponsor:	Brooks Foundation, Gladys
URL:	http://www.gladysbrooksfoundation.org/guidelines.html
Sponsor Type:	Private foundation
Amount:	$50,000
Upper Amount:	$100,000
Deadline:	June 1, 2010. Electronic submissions are not acceptable.
Amount Note:	Grant applications will be considered only for major expenditures between $50,000 and $100,000 and greater or lesser amounts in certain circumstances.
Activity Location:	Connecticut, Delaware, Florida, Illinois, Louisiana, Maine, Maryland, Massachusetts, New Hampshire, New Jersey, New York, Ohio, Pennsylvania, Rhode Island, Tennessee, Vermont
Citizenship or Residency:	United States
Requirements:	Nonprofit

Abstract:	Grant activities in the field of libraries will be considered generally for resource endowments (print, film, electronic database, speakers/workshops), capital construction, and innovative equipment. Projects fostering broader public access to global information sources utilizing collaborative efforts, pioneering technologies, and equipment are encouraged.
Eligibility:	The foundation will make grants only to publicly supported not-for-profit, tax-exempt libraries.
COS Keywords:	Library Science
Funding Type:	Equipment or materials acquisition or facility use; facility construction or operation.
Sponsor contact information:	Gladys Brooks Foundation 1055 Franklin Ave., Suite 208 Garden City, NY 11530
Bookmark URL:	http://fundingopps.cos.com/cgi-bin/fo2/getRec?id=59197

SAMPLE 2

This sample is modified from COS Funding Opportunities (accessed 22 February 2010).

COS Unique ID:	106840
Date Last Revised:	March 18, 2009, 12:00 AM
Title:	Therapeutic Effects of Horses on Humans
Sponsor:	Horses and Humans Foundation
URL:	http://www.horsesandhumans.org
Sponsor Type:	Other nonprofit
Upper Amount:	$100,000
Deadline:	May 15, 2010. Electronic submissions are not acceptable.
Amount Note:	Grants are generally a maximum of $100,000 awarded for up to a one-year period.
Activity Location:	Unrestricted
Requirements:	Nonprofit
Abstract:	Grant activities considered for research related to improving the understanding of the therapeutic effects of riding on handicapped rehabilitation. Eligibility: PhD/MD/Other Professional
COS Keywords:	Handicapped Rehabilitation Physical Medicine and Rehabilitation

Funding Type:	Research
Sponsor contact information:	Horses and Humans Research Foundation
	PO Box 480
	Chagrin Falls, OH 44022
Bookmark URL:	http://fundingopps.cos.com/cgi-bin/fo2/getRec?id =106840

Appendix E: Sample Organizational Chart

Jamestown Literacy Volunteers Organizational Chart

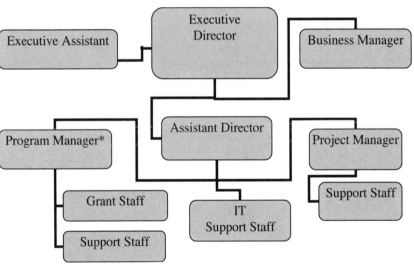

* Program manager will serve as project director.

Appendix F:
Grant-writing Worksheets

EXAMPLE 1: GRANT-WRITING WORKSHEET FOR
PRELIMINARY, PREAPPLICATION WORK

Tentative Title of Your Grant Project:

Who is the one person responsible for the grant?

What do you want (e.g., computers, furniture, construction, programming support for presenters)?

Why do you need this (e.g., to improve student reading scores, to have more current technology available to library patrons, to teach others how to search for jobs)?

How will you evaluate this project (surveys, increase in access to a number of databases, more current average copyright date, increase in the number of people using a service, etc.)?

List organizations that you can partner with:

List potential funders (e.g., grants, foundations):

How will you continue this project when funding ends?

How will you recognize funders (check presentation, press releases, grand opening, etc.)?

What supporting documentation do you need?

- Letters of support
- Organization's mission statement
- Brief organizational history
- List of board members
- Bylaws
- Financial statement (990)
- Federal tax ID number
- Demographics of your service population
- Statistics on use of services
- Testimonials
- Resumes of key staff personnel

EXAMPLE 2: GRANT-WRITING WORKSHEET FOR WRITING FINAL PROPOSAL

Date:
Title of the Project:
$ Amount Requested: $

I. Contact Information

Name: (Name of project director)
Title: (Project director's official title)
Organization's name:
Address:
Phone number:
Fax Number:
E-mail address:
Web address:
Organization's federal tax ID number:

II. Brief Overview of Proposed Project

Title of the Project:
Summary or Abstract of the Project: Provide a brief explanation of the proposed project. Address the "Five Ws": who, what, when, where, and why, as well as the dollar amount being requested.

III. Background Information about the Organization

Provide the following information in this section:

- Mission statement
- Vision statement
- Brief history of the organization
- Main goals of the organization's current strategic plan with reference on how to access the complete strategic plan
- Identification of the population you serve and current usage data
- List of a few recently successful projects that the organization has completed

IV. Information about the Project

In this section, complete the following and answer the following questions:

- Why is your project important?
  - ○ Provide qualitative and quantitative data from surveys, focus groups, interviews, etc.
  - ○ Reference expert opinion, research studies, etc.
- What are you going to do (specific action items, activities, purchases, etc.) with the funding that you receive? Provide a timeline of activities in a table or chart format.
- Who are your partners? (If applicable).
- What do you specifically hope to accomplish?
- Explain how your project meets the goals of the grant.
- Identify explicitly how your project directly addresses the goals of the granting agency or foundation.
- Explain the positive impact that your project will have on a specific group.
- Specify how this project will continue after grant funding ends.

V. Budget Narrative

- Provide a proposed budget in spreadsheet format.
- Explain each budget item, including cost per item and how it is to be paid for (in-kind support, grant funding, other funding, etc.).
- Explain what in-kind support that your organization will be providing to the project.
- Provide a brief explanation of other sources of revenue or in-kind support from partnering organizations, groups, etc.

VI. Evaluation and Information Sharing

- How will you evaluate this project?
- What evaluation measures will you use to determine whether or not you have achieved project goals?
- Specifically indicate how you will share information about the project (press releases, presentations, etc.).

VII. Appendices

- Provide a list of current board members, including officers.
- Provide a reference to updated bylaws.
- Provide a copy of the organization's most recent financial statement (also known as the "990").
- Include a list of references used to develop the proposal (books, articles, etc.).

Appendix G: Case Study #1: Sample Narrative of a Successful Grant

One reason that this grant was successful is that the narrative provided in the application addressed the items as outlined in the grant guidelines. This included (a) clearly defining the purpose of the grant; (b) specifying criteria used to determine the scope of the project; (c) reference to expert studies, research, and opinions; and (d) a detailed explanation of the role of each participant in the project.

FROM THE ABSTRACT

The purpose of this grant is to promote the development of information discovery skills, increase student reading achievement, and encourage lifelong reading through the implementation of a library-based reading improvement project that targets first- and second-grade students. This project serves to help meet the school district's goal of all children reading on grade level by the third grade through providing professional development opportunities to teachers and school media specialists in the areas of children's literature, collaboration, and technology; expanding the size of the school library collection to increase the ratio of volumes to students; and adding computer workstations for increased access to information by students, teachers, and parents.

FROM THE "NEED" SECTION

An extensive review of all elementary schools in the district was required to make an equitable decision as to which schools would become project

Table G.1. Factors Considered during the Selection Process

School Name & District	Poverty Level	Total Enrollment	TAAS Reading Passing Rate	Collection Size	# Average Copyright Date	Computers Per Student	Books Per Student
	95	1067	53	9558	1985	5	9
	93	677	50	4514	1991	2	7
	100	557	12	5030	1991	1	9
	94	501	12	6932	1989	3	14

participants. The following criteria were used to identify project schools: Texas Assessment of Academic Skills (TAAS) Reading percent passing rate, size and age of library collection, books-per-student ratio, number of computers for student use, presence of a certified school media specialist/librarian on site, enrollment per school, and poverty level per school. Information was gathered via campus visits, analysis of inventory lists, and completion of an online analysis of the library collections. Table G.1 shows the factors considered during the selection process.

ACQUISITION OF BOOKS AND MATERIALS

Studies have shown that when students have an extensive collection of books to choose from, reading scores increase. Through this grant, each participating school will receive a minimum of 500 books to increase the volume-per-student ratio.

TECHNOLOGY

For students to be effective users of technology, they must have access to computers to practice such skills as information discovery and retrieval. Through this project, the selected campuses would receive four workstations in the library to lower the student-to-computer ratio and facilitate information discovery skills through the use of online resources.

SCIENTIFIC-BASED RESEARCH AND REPORTS

There has been an explosion of research conducted in the last few decades that supports the critical elements of an effective school program. Those elements are: collaboration, reading achievement, access to an adequate collection, enhanced technology, and expanded hours of library operation. (See list of references to these topics included at the end of this grant package.)

The school media center/library is at the heart of the school. It is the place where democracy reigns because students are free to access books and information; where students learn to read for enjoyment as well as for knowledge; and where analysis, synthesis, evaluation, and communication are encouraged. The library is a place where students can practice their technology skills with the assistance and support of the librarian.

School libraries' contribution to information literacy and student achievement is documented in the following essential elements of its programming.

Explanation of Participants' Roles: The success of the grant depends on the coordination and involvement of all participants. Participants and their duties are as follows:

Library Media Specialist (LMS)/Site Administrator: The library media specialist will be the on-site administrator for this grant. The LMS is expected to:

- Collaborate with teachers in lesson planning by integrating new skills and techniques with the district's curriculum.
- Communicate with grant coordinators and keep the school informed of grant developments.
- Facilitate and implement professional development training into the library program.

Teachers:

- Participate in all professional development activities associated with the grant.
- Implement new skills and techniques into their lessons.
- Compile a list of titles and materials in collaboration with LMS to enhance the library collection.

School Administrator:

- Communicate biweekly with LMS, teachers, and grant administrators regarding the grant and its initiatives.
- Help monitor grant initiatives.

Grant Director/Administrator:

- Oversee the administration of the grant.
- Oversee the installation of technology equipment in support of the project.

Parents:

- Participate in events related to grant initiatives on Parents' Night.
- Use the school library's technology resources.

Community: The Madison Public Library will support the project by:

- Providing public library cards to parents, students, and teachers.
- Informing the school community about its programming and resources.
- Providing a tour of the neighborhood public library.

Evaluation: To ensure maximum effectiveness of the project, both formative and summative evaluations will be implemented throughout the life cycle of the grant. This project will be evaluated through the collection analysis, usage statistics on online resources, parent and teacher surveys. Adjustments to programming will be made according to input from the site administrator's monthly reports.

Appendix H: Case Study #2: Sample Narrative from an Unsuccessful Grant

One reason that this grant was unsuccessful is that the narrative failed to address the items as outlined in the grant guidelines. This narrative did not talk about the following: (a) specifying tangible outcomes (e.g., how much student performance will improve and what performance measures will be used); and (b) reference to expert studies, research, and opinion. Additionally, grammatical and spelling errors appear throughout the narrative.

PROGRAM DESCRIPTION

The district has researched educational programs and services used successfully in the Sate [*sic*] and nationally with specific emphasis on the needs expressed herein. As a result, the Rural Academic Portfolio (REAP) and the Accelerated Reading program (AR) have been identified. READ and AR comprise a suite of educational software designed for the special needs of districts such as ours.

REAP is compiled and provided by EduEquity, Inc., a nationally recognized provider of educational solutions to demographically challenged districts.

AR is compiled and provided by Renaissance Learning Inc. It has a positive effect on student achievement, especially for socioeconomically disadvantage childs [*sic*]. It is a system of computerized testing and record-keeping with a goal to increased literature-based reading practice.

This application is for the purpose of obtaining funds for the purchase of the READ and AR programs for use by students.

We will also need funds for twelve computers which will be set up in our elementary library to handle the programs and give students access.

ACTION PLAN (USE OF FUNDS)

We will purchase and install 12 computer stations in the Watson Elementary School library which will be used by the students for REAP, AR, and research. Our results will be: Improved student performance, improved attendance, reduced discipline and behavior problems, increased awareness about student career choices, and improved accountability with expelled and suspended students. Training and experiences by teachers and support personnel with instructional software alternatives.

The program will be evaluated with pre- and post-testing, data generated via the software, format testing, behavior records and observations, and interviews with teachers and parents related to empirical and behavioral changes due to program interventions.

Appendix I: Examples of Needs Assessments

EXAMPLE 1

This is an example of a needs assessment that was completed and included in a grant application seeking funding to improve information resources and library services.

Table I.1. Example of Needs Assessment to Improve Information Resources

Area of Importance	Needs Assessment
Library Hours	The library is only open during regular school days and hours. Library services and information resources are not available after school, on weekends, or during the summer.
Media Specialist— Teacher Collaboration	Communication and collaborative efforts are not coordinated between the teachers and the school media specialist. Of specific concern is the lack of coordinated programming to teach information discovery skills to K–3 students.
Nonprint Resources	The average copyright date of nonprint resources such as DVDs, CDs, videos, microforms, etc. is 1980. Outdated and in poor condition, these important educational resources are not aligned with local, state, or federal education standards.
Print Resources	The average copyright date of resources in print, both fiction and nonfiction, is 1985. Students minimally use the book collection due to the fact that the average copyright date is 20+ years old.

(continued)

Table I.1. (*continued*)

Area of Importance	Needs Assessment
Professional Development Opportunities	Professional development opportunities in the area of teaching information discovery skills and its integration into the curriculum is minimal. Additional funding is not anticipated.
Reading Standards	More than 45% of third-grade students fall below the 50th percentile on the SAT 9 test. The entire school district has an API score of 950, which is well below the state average of 1046.

EXAMPLE 2

This is an example of a needs assessment that was completed and included in a grant application seeking funding to expand an equine rescue/equine therapy program.

Table I.2.   Example of a Needs Assessment for a Therapeutic Riding Program

Area of Concern	Needs Assessment Results
Need for additional hay	It takes 35 bales of hay daily to feed the 10 horses in the program. Cost-benefit assessment results show a cost savings for hay of 20% if the organization purchases the 25 acres adjacent to the facility.
Assisting riders in getting on and off horses.	Four people are needed to assist a physically challenged rider to get on and off a horse. Purchasing the equipment to assist in mounting will release two people to assist other riders.
Website development	A survey of the 350 program participants revealed that an expanded website that includes scheduling information, news updates, referral information, etc. would greatly facilitate communication.
Classroom space	Interviews with area colleges and universities that partner with the organization indicate that a classroom on the property would enable more students to learn about equine-assisted therapy.

Appendix J: Example of an Unsuccessful Budget

Table J.1 is an example of an unsuccessful budget narrative. Note that this narrative was included in a grant application that provided the following guidelines: (a) funds cannot be used for travel or attendance at conferences; (b) funds cannot be used to pay for an outside evaluator; (c) supplies must be listed per item, quantity, and estimated cost.

Table J.1.   Example of an Unsuccessful Budget Narrative

Line Items	Specifics	Funds Needed
Personnel: Director, $100,000 Assistant, $20,000	Example: 20% of time 35% of time	Subtotal: $20,000 $7,000 Total personnel: $27,000
Fringe Benefits: Est. rate of 24%	Example: 24% Dir. and Assist.	Subtotal: $6,480
Travel: National conference	Cost per employee: $2,000	Total: $4,000
Equipment: Computers	2 wireless laptops at $3,000/ea.	Total: $6,000
Supplies: Books: $40,000 Supplies: $10,000 LCD projector 2— $1,000/each	10,000 books	Total: Books: $40,000 Supplies: $10,000 LCD projectors: $2,000 Library shelving: $10,000 Total: $62,000
Contracts: Evaluation	Third-party evaluator, 5 days = $30,000	$30,000

Appendix K: Example of a Successful Budget

Table K.1 is an example of a successful budget narrative. Note that this narrative was included in a grant application that provided the following guidelines: (a) personnel costs must show fringe benefit costs separate from salary costs; (b) library system training (if applied for) must be listed under the "contractual" category; and (c) library books and materials must be listed under "supplies."

Table K.1. Example of a Successful Budget Narrative Budget Category

Line Items	Specific Information Regarding Line Item	Funds Requested	
1. Personnel	Media Center Staff: 1,392 total hours of work at 5 target sites @ $25.00 per hour		$34,800
	Project Director: 340 hours of work @ $27.50 per hour		$9,350
		Total Personnel:	$44,150
2. Fringe Benefits	FICA: 7.65%		$3,377
	Matching retirement: 5.815%		$2,567
		Total Fringe Benefits:	$5,944
3. Equipment	26 IBM PCs for Internet stations @ $1,100 each		$28,600

(*continued*)

Table K.1. (*continued*)

Line Items	Specific Information Regarding Line Item	Funds Requested	
4. Supplies	Integrated library system		$41,800
	Library books for 5 target sites		$95,000
		Total Supplies:	$136,800
5. Contractual	Evaluation		$10,000
	Library system training		$13,500
		Total Contracts:	$ 23,500
Grand Total			$210,394

Appendix L: Examples of Evaluation Plans

EXAMPLE 1: EVALUATION PLAN FOR THE "READING ON THE ROAD" PROJECT

This is a basic example of an evaluation plan for a literacy program called "Reading on the Road." Success of the project, in part, will be determined by comparing reading scores of project participants. The project will be considered extremely successful if each project participant raises his or her reading score by three points. Evaluation outcomes will be used to write an analysis of the successes and challenges of the project for the final project report.

Table L.1. Sample Evaluation Plan, "Reading on the Road"

Area of Evaluation	Evaluation Instrument	Evaluation Outcome
Literary Skills	Pretesting when participant begins program. Post-testing when participant completes the program.	Comparison of pretest and post-test scores of each participant.
Participant Perceptions	Web survey distributed to project participants after program completed.	Analysis of Web survey results including quantitative and qualitative data.
	Exit interviews conducted after participants complete the program	Content analysis of exit interviews.

EXAMPLE 2: EVALUATION PLAN FOR THE "CURRENT COLLECTIONS" PROJECT

This is an example of an evaluation plan for a library collection-building program called "Current Collections." Success of the project will be determined by the increase of copyright date for the library collection, an increase in the number of books borrowed from the library, and analyzing quantitative and qualitative information from survey results of library users. This project will be considered successful if the average copyright date moves from 1980 to 2005, if circulation statistics increase by 5 percent, and if feedback from the surveys is positive. Evaluation outcomes will be used to write an analysis of the successes and challenges of the project for the final project report.

Table L.2.   Sample Evaluation Plan, "Current Collections"

Area of Evaluation	Evaluation Instrument	Evaluation Outcome
Currency of the library book collection	Collection analysis for copyright uses the library's integrated library system four weeks before the end of the grant cycle.	Average copyright date of the collection.
Usage of the library book collection	Circulation statistics gathered for one week, some time during the final month of the project.	Number of books circulated should increase at least 5% when compared to the number of books circulated at the beginning of the project.
Library users' perceptions	Web survey distributed via e-mail to library users.	75% of the quantitative results should be at the "improved" or "much improved" level. 80% of the qualitative responses should have one positive comment.

Appendix M: Sample Grant Application Form for a Foundation

Modified from the Grant Application Form required by the Western New York Foundation, 4050 Harlem Rd., Snyder, NY 14226

1. Name of Agency:
   Address:
   City:
   State:
   ZIP code:
   Phone number:
   Fax number:
   E-mail address:
   Website:
   Date of application:
   Name of contact person:

FACTUAL INFORMATION

2. Amount of Request: $
3. Total Cost of Project: $
4. Project Description (one or two sentences):
5. Date of Board Vote Authorizing This Request:
6. Date of IRS Tax Exemption Letter (attach copy):
7. Tax ID Number:
8. Is agency a member of the United Way?
9. If yes, is the United Way aware of this request?

10. Government funds and grants in most recent fiscal year: (Attach additional pages as needed). For each, include:
    - Source
    - Purpose
    - Amount
11. Have you had any contact with a trustee on this request? If yes, please provide the name of the trustee:
12. Have you applied to any other foundations for all or part of the cost of this project? (Attach additional pages as needed). For each include:
    - Date
    - Foundation
    - Amount
    - Response
    - Amount granted
13. What requests for funds have you made to other foundations during the past 18 months? Please provide their names, the project, the amount requested, the cost of the project, and the amount granted.
14. How many nongovernment dollars does your board raise yearly?

REQUIRED DOCUMENTATION

1. The Argument: In one to three pages, provide a description of the project and the reasons why this project is important, including costs and benefits. Address the question: Why should the foundation make a grant to your organization? If the request for funding is only a partial request of the total project cost, or if this foundation grants you a portion of your request, explain how the balance of funds will be raised. Please include the numbers of individuals who will benefit from your project, as well as operating cost savings or increases that will occur if this project is implemented.
2. Collaboration: How have you considered collaboration with other agencies?
3. Project Evaluation: How will you evaluate the success or failure of this project?
4. Exhibits: Although not required, include any exhibits to strengthen your case.

FINANCIAL INFORMATION

The following information must be included with your application:

A. Audited annual report for the last fiscal year or unaudited if not available.

B. Current year budget and operating costs to date.
C. Financial projections highlighting any changes that will occur if this project is implemented.

ORGANIZATIONAL INFORMATION

The following information must be included with your application:

A. A current list of the board of directors, including their occupations.
B. Literature on the agency, including the most recent executive director's report.
C. Copy of the board president's most recent report (top board officer, not a staff member).

BIDS FOR SERVICES

If you are requesting funds to purchase equipment or services that cost more than $5,000 each, include three competitive bids with this application.

CERTIFICATION

This application must be signed by the executive director and the current board president.

I (We) hereby certify that should our request for funding be approved, the funds received from the Western New York Foundation will be used for the purposes requested, and no other; and at the end of one year from the date of this request, a report on the progress of the grant will be provided to the Executive Director.

Date:
Name of Executive Director:
Signature of the Executive Director:

Date:
Name of Board President:
Signature of Board President:

References

American Grant Writers Association
   http://www.agwa.us/
American Library Association
   http://www.ala.org
Buffalo Hearing and Speech Center
   http://askbhsc.org
Chronicle of Philanthropy
   http://philanthropy.com
Chronicle of Philanthropy Guide to Grants
   http://philanthropy.com/grants/
Council of Nonprofits
   http://www.councilofnonprofits.org
COS—Community of Science (subunit of ProQuest)
   http://www.cos.com/
Database of State Incentives for Renewable Energy
   http://www.dsireusa.org
Fieldstone Farm Therapeutic Riding Center
   http://www.fieldstonefarmtrc.com/
Foundation Center, *Foundation Directory Online*
   http://fconline.fdncenter.org/
Foundation Center, *Grants to Individuals Online*
   http://gtionline.foundationcenter.org/
Foundations
   http://www.foundations.org
Grants.gov
   http://www.grants.gov

James Addison Jones Library, Greensboro College
      http://www.greensborocollege.edu/library/
Karsh, Ellen, and Arlen Sue Fox, *The Only Grant-Writing Book You'll Ever
      Need*. New York: Carroll & Graf Publishers, 2003.
National Center for Charitable Statistics
      http://nccs.urban.org
Niagara Falls Neighborhood Housing Services, Inc.
      http://nfs.nw.org/report/nworeport_printaspx?orgid=8074
Nonprofit Connect: Network, Learn, Grow
      http://www.npconnect.com
Office of Management and Budget
      http://earmarks.omb.gov/2008_appropriations_earmarks_110th
      _congress.html
Philanthropy Journal
      http://www.philanthropyjournal.org
SPIN: Sponsored Program Information Network
      http://ww1.infoed.org/
SurveyMonkey
      http://www.surveymonkey.com

Additional Resources

American Library Association website (search under "grants")
www.ala.org

Bray, Ilona. *Effective Fundraising for Nonprofits: Real-world Strategies That Work.* Berkeley, CA: Nolo Press, 2008.

Brannock, Jennifer. "The NEH preservation assistance grant: A funding opportunity for first time grant writers." *Mississippi Libraries* 71, no. 3 (Fall 2007): 65–66.

Brooks, Douglas. "Grant writing for beginners: Part 1." *Technology & Learning* 28, no. 6 (January 2008): 34.

Brooks, Douglas. "Grant writing for beginners: Part 2." *Technology & Learning* 28, no. 7 (February 2008): 34.

Brooks, Douglas. "Grant writing for beginners: Part 3." *Technology & Learning* 28, no. 8 (February 2008): 38.

Burnett, Sara. "In search of grant money." *Community College Week* 19, no. 22 (July 16, 2007): 8.

Conway, Ashlie. "The music librarian as development officer: Raising funds for special collections." *Music Reference Services Quarterly* 11, nos. 3/4 (2008): 203–28.

"eSchool News"
www.eschoolnews.com/

FastWEB
www.fastweb.com

Federal Resources for Educational Excellence (FREE)
www.ed.gov/free/

Forum for Regional Associations of Grantmakers
www.givingforum.org

Franklin, P., and Claire G. Stephens. "Gaining skills to write winning grants." *School Library Media Activities Monthly* 25 no. 3 (November 2008): 43–44.

Fundsnet Online Services
www.fundsnetservices.com

Grantionary
www.eduplace.com/grants/help/grantionary.html

GrantsAlert
www.grantsalert.com

Grantsmanship Center.
www.tgci.com/STATES/states2.htm

Hall, Mary Stuart, and Susan Howlett. *Getting Funded: The Complete Guide to Writing Grant Proposals.* Portland, OR: Portland University Press, 2003.

Himes, A. C. "A formula for successful grant writing: Four proven keys." *Academic Leader* 22, no. 3 (March 2006): 4–8.

Hindley, Meredith. "How to get a grant from NEH." *Humanities* 29, no. 4 (July/August 2008): 47–49.

Improving Literacy through School Libraries (federal grant)
http://www.ed.gov/programs/lsl/index.html

Information Today. *Big Book of Library Grant Money.* Chicago: ALA, 2007.

Institute of Museum and Library Services
www.imls.gov

Kerney, Carol. "Inside the mind of a grant reader." *Technology & Learning* 25, no. 11 (June 2005): 62–66.

Lemmon, Kathryn. "How to begin grant writing." *Writer* 120, no. 11 (November 2007): 13.

National Endowment for the Humanities
http://www.neh.gov/grants/index.html

Philanthropy News Digest
http://foundationcenter.org/pnd/

Pippard, Debbie. "How to . . . access big funding." *Green Places* no. 58 (September 2009): 34–35.

Porter, Robert. "Why academics have a hard time writing good grant proposals."*Journal of Research Administration* 38, no. 2 (2007): 161–67.

Primer, Ben. "Resources for archives: Developing collections, constituents, colleagues, and capital." *Journal of Archival Organization* 7, nos. 1/2 (January 2009): 58–65.

Radeschi, Loretta. "Dissecting the grant review process." *Crafts Report* 32 (April 2007): 28–29.

Reese, Susan. "Grant writing 101." *Techniques: Connecting Education and Careers* 80, no. 4 (April 2005): 24–27.

Sand, Michael A., and Linda Lysakowski. *The Essential Nonprofit Fundraising Handbook.* Franklin Lakes, NJ: Career Press, 2009.

Technology Grant News
  www.technologygrantnews.com
Technology Grant News, ed. *Winning at IT: Grant Writing for Technology Grants [2009]*. New York: Technology Grant News, 2009.
"Taking the lead on grant writing." *Techniques: Connecting Education and Careers* 83, no. 1 (January 2008): 9–10.
Williams, Shannon. "Strategies for writing winning proposals: A proactive approach to grant seeking." *Tennessee Libraries* (online) 58, no. 2 (2008): 1–6. http://www.tnla.org (accessed 22 February 2010).

OTHER GOOD GRANT SITES

Deborah Kluge's Proposalwriter.com
  www.proposalwriter.com
Friends of Libraries USA (lists fund-raising ideas)
  www.folusa.org
GrantProposal.com
  www.grantproposal.com (useful grant writing tips)
HP Global Social Development. K–16 grants, grants for higher education. Primarily for science and technology-related/teaching projects
  http://grants.hp.com
Library Support Staff. "Fundraising for Libraries: Links and Resources"
  http://www.librarysupportstaff.com/find$.html
Mid-Hudson Library System. "Fundraising: Grant Makers" (links to program grants, collection/preservation grants/construction grants, etc.)
  http://midhudson.org/funding/fundraising/grantmakers.htm
Michigan State University. "Grants for Nonprofits: Libraries" (list of grants for libraries)
  www.lib.msu.edu/harris23/grants/2lib.htm
New York State Energy Research and Development Authority (search under "Municipal—New Construction Program")
  http://www.nyserda.org/incentives.asp
Non-Profit Guides (gives sample [generic] grant proposals)
  www.npguides.org
The Grantsmanship Center, Inc. (TGCI) website (provides sample grants)
  www.tcgigrantproposals.com

Index

About the Author

Gail M. Staines, MLS, PhD, is assistant provost for university libraries at Saint Louis University, St. Louis, Missouri. Gail has twenty-plus years of grant-writing experience with a 99 percent grant-procurement rate. Previously, she served as the executive director of the Western New York Library Resources Council and as visiting lecturer, University of Buffalo, Department of Library and Information Studies. Named a "Mover & Shaker" in 2004 by *Library Journal*, Gail is a frequent presenter and offers workshops on grant writing. An author of several articles, she is also the coauthor of *Social Sciences Research: Research, Writing, and Presentation Strategies for Students* (2008).